Step-families

Step-families

a cooperative responsibility

by Fredrick Capaldi
and Barbara McRae

NEW VIEWPOINTS / VISION BOOKS
A division of Franklin Watts
New York / London / 1979

To our parents

In loving memory of my mother,
Emogene Capaldi.

ACKNOWLEDGMENTS

We wish to thank our friends and colleagues who offered support and understanding: Dr. Paul Wood, Dr. Alice Pitman, and Curly Johnson. Special thanks to Mary Reeves who was instrumental in getting the manuscript to the publisher and for having typed the finished product. Most of all, we wish to thank the hundreds of students, parents, children, and clients who attended our courses and shared with us their experiences.

NEW VIEWPOINTS/VISION BOOKS
A Division of Franklin Watts
730 Fifth Avenue
New York, New York 10019

Library of Congress Cataloging in Publication Data

Capaldi, Fredrick.
  Stepfamilies.

  Bibliography: p.
  Includes index.
  1. Stepchildren—United States. 2. Stepparents—United States. 3. Remarriage—United States.
I. McRae, Barbara, joint author. II. Title.
HQ777.7.C26   301.42'7   79-9342
ISBN 0-531-06750-5 pbk.
    0-531-06373-9

Table of Contents

Preface

One of the oldest living institutions is the family. Since the beginning of time, men and women have joined to create family systems. Both male and female members worked toward a common goal: the perpetuation of the family. They strived to form a loving, nurturing system that would endure over the years through the children.

Throughout the Western world, a husband and wife's work as parents included teaching their offspring acceptable social behaviors and encouraging mutual support among family members. Mother and father cared for the physical and mental needs of their children. In return for this sustenance, the children offered love, respect, and obedience. Both parents and children attempted to set up a supportive, comfortable family system. Father and mother governed the family unit; the children carried out their parents' wishes.

Many families today strive to maintain this Western traditional family system with little success. Mother and father experience problems in the relationship as husband and wife. This troubled relationship affects the children. Over time, the family breaks up.

A natural result of the breakdown of the original family is the eventual formation of the stepfamily. This family differs—

1

a man or a woman assumes the responsibility for helping to raise another person's children.

Most of us have been conditioned to want our own children, not someone else's. Time may change, customs may change ... but people don't change in this attitude. Most people still want their own children. Caring for another's children— the steprelationship—still promotes uneasy, uncomfortable feelings for family members.

A major factor contributing to these feelings is the lack of a model for steppeople. Today we have models to assist us in becoming proficient in just about everything, but there is no model on how to "make it" in the blended family. This book constructs such a model for stepfamilies—a positive approach to living in step. The book not only outlines the problems inherent in the blended family, but also offers positive alternatives to bring about a cohesive, supportive blended family: exploration of the unrealistic expectations, definition of roles, communication, and planning.

Until recently, steppeople seeking support, reassurance, and help had two options: (1) to read the literature written concerning the steprelationship; (2) to participate in counseling. Both of these options were not without pitfalls.

The search for helpful literature was often fruitless; until this past year, there were only about nine books that dealt with the perils and problems of steppeople. The books offered little help and few answers.

As one stepmother remarked, "Reading three books about stepfamilies has succeeded in scaring me to death about marrying my boyfriend. He has custody of his two sons, and I just don't know if I can handle the situation. None of the books I read gave me any help!"

Most of the early texts were written by stepmothers who had encountered difficulties in their own stepfamilies. They used this difficult experience as the basis for their book. No one in a frustrating family situation needs or wants to hear only about the problems someone else had in the same situation. Instead, they want solutions.

Seeking help in arriving at solutions, many steppeople have pursued the second option, professional counseling. The pitfall lies in the selection of professional assistance, a process with which the average person is inexperienced. In selecting professional help, it is vitally important to ascertain that the therapist one is consulting indeed has had training and experience in family therapy and is not someone who specializes in one-to-one treatment. Indeed, the therapist should have specific training and knowledge of blended families.

As family therapists specializing in working with stepfamilies, we have tried to write this book from an objective point of view. The aim of the book is to fill a void in the needs of single parents considering remarriage and in the needs of blended families. We have developed an effective alternative for dealing with stepfamily problems. It's not instant; it's not easy; and it's not magic. It is, however, an effective tool for parents to use in working together to achieve a successful stepfamily.

The purpose of our book is to assist stepparents and stepchildren in gaining a better understanding of those problems that beleaguer them, and to guide them toward a successful resolution. The reality is that most successful stepfamilies are strong, cohesive families filled with warmth and caring. These stepfamilies arrived at their success through the unceasing and untiring efforts of their members. In this book, we hope to aid other stepfamilies achieve success in their endeavors toward family unity.

Introduction

The steprelationship is not a new phenomenon; it is, however, an ever-increasing one. Over one third of this country's population exists in this family system of his, hers, mine, and ours. Across the nation last year, there were 2,193,000 marriages and 1,105,000 divorces. The average family had 2.86 children under eighteen years of age. This means that each year, there are a growing number of single-parent families. And, concurrently, there are many single parents remarrying.

Many newly divorced parents emphatically declare, "Statistics don't include me . . . I don't even want to think about marrying again!"

Yet estimates are that almost 75 percent of single parents *do* remarry, most within three years; and that means the creation of stepfamilies.

Unfortunately, a great number of these blended families founder. Why? To understand stepfamily function, one must understand the unique experiences and people involved in the steprelationship.

The *single parent* has gone through a major life crisis—death or divorce—and experienced a subsequent period of adjustment. This period of adjustment to life as a single parent is called the interim period. It may be a relatively short period of time or a long period of time. It may have been used constructively as an opportunity for growth and deeper emotional maturity, or it may have been siezed on as an excuse for emotional and physical stagnation.

The reasons for constructive or destructive behavior during the interim period may be varied. Some individuals who choose to stagnate may do so out of fear of the unknown future. They may stagnate out of ignorance of the options open to them, the opportunities for growth. Or they may lack the financial resources to smooth the road to increased growth; it requires money to take advantage of growth opportunities. Stagnation can be prevented by education and opportunities available to single parents, by financial assistance available through colleges and government, and by practical aids such as day care centers and single-parent organizations such as Parents Without Partners.

Many new *stepparents* may expect the new marriage to solve all the old problems, or at least make life's problems easier to deal with. Others proceed to remarry, optimistically, knowing that blending two families will not be easy but confident that they will prevail over any difficulties. The many possible variations in the stepfamily illustrate the complexity involved. There is the stepfamily in which one single parent has children and marries an individual who has never been married or never had children. Or consider the stepfamily in which both parents have children by a previous marriage or, in some cases, marriages. There are additional variations. One, the manner in which the single parent became a single parent—death of a spouse or divorce—is important. The death of a spouse is extremely traumatic and involves shock, denial, mourning, and adjustment. Divorces are rarely truly amiable or easily forgotten. The emotional scars remain for a long time. Two, the custody arrangements and financial agreements settled on by the divorcing adults carry important implications for the future stepfamily. Dr. David Rogers found in his study of steppeople that finances are the biggest problem for remarrieds and that visitation rights are an emotionally draining experience for stepfamilies. More will be said about all of these factors later in the book.

The *children* in a stepfamily are the third consideration. The age of the children involved in the blended family greatly affects the ease of transition from two families to one stepfamily. The younger the children, generally, the easier or quicker the success. The older the children still living at home—specifically adolescents—the more difficult the task. Regardless of age, however, all children have experienced the breakup of the parents' marriage or the death of a parent. They have experienced the changes of the interim period—that time of adjustment following their parents' divorce and preceding their full acceptance of a new life-style. Many children never fully accept the divorce, harboring feelings of blame for the parents' breaking up and wondering years later why it happened. The children must oftentimes adjust to the diminished role in their lives of the parent without full-time custody, the absentee parent. And finally, the children in a newly formed stepfamily must learn to gracefully include a new adult in their family circle, an adult who has a very special relationship to their parent and to themselves.

All of these steppeople—single parent, stepparent, and stepchildren—must somehow blend and deal with the following issues to avoid becoming part of that 47 percent failure statistic.

The first major issue occurs for single parents and stepchildren during the interim period. Success as a stepfamily will not be possible unless single parents, absentee parents, and children experience a healthy adjustment to the changes encountered in the interim period. A healthy adjustment during the interim period encompasses coping with the death of the spouse/parent and acceptance of this loss; it may mean coping with the divorce from a spouse or between one's parents and an acceptance of this divorce as final and inevitable with no one at fault. A healthy adjustment also encompasses the creation of a new single-parent family system and life-style that is comfortable for all members. It involves the creation of a life-style that includes the absentee parent as a vital yet separate part of the child's life. A healthy adjustment during the interim period means a psychologically healthy individual entering into the steprelationship.

The second major issue that must be dealt with by single parent, stepparent, and stepchildren occurs just prior to the remarriage and in the early stages of the formation of the stepfamily. All steppeople have expectations—realistic and unrealistic—as they enter into the steprelationship. They harbor hopes, dreams, fears, and information regarding what it will be like. They may expect that people will behave a certain way or that the future will have certain destined outcomes. A common way of thinking among stepparents who have never had children is the *instant parent* expectation. Although this instant parent has never had children, he or she believes that he or she will know just how to parent (unrealistic!). On the other hand, the natural parent may be the one who staunchly maintains that the stepparent will know just how to parent (unrealistic!), while the stepparent worries that it's not going to be all that easy! (Realistic!) The interesting thing about unrealistic expectations—few people verbalize, share and discuss these expectations prior to the remarriage. Time and time again, when left unexplored, the unrealistic expectations slip out to trip up family relationships. They trip up relationships for the simple reason that when someone in the family doesn't behave as another expects, or the future doesn't bring what someone expects, resentment builds and finally explodes. It's vitally important to openly share expectations and explore their realistic and unrealistic aspects to prevent such an explosion. This exploration could be done at weekly "family" gatherings prior to the actual remarriage and then incorporated as a family tradition after the blending of families has taken place.

The third issue to be faced by stepfamilies are the myths that surround the steprelationship, such as "wicked stepparent" and "instant love." The stepparent is often seen by others as somehow mean and cruel, not quite as good as the real parent. Both stepmother and stepfather often feel on trial, as if they must prove themselves to be a good parent. The stepparents often feel pressured to feel instant love—they must immediately love their new spouse's children simply because they love the children's parent. This love for one's stepchildren is something that cannot be forced. Success in the steprelationship involves liking. Hopefully, the stepparent may get to know the stepchild or stepchildren well and feel a genuine liking for them; but he or she does not have to instantly love the children. The fortunate stepparent and stepchild may grow to love one another over time, a slow and natural process, one that is not forced. Or the feelings may comfortably remain at mutual respect and friendship.

The fourth issue to be dealt with by successfully blended families centers around the definition and clarification of roles. All family members bring to the steprelationship their own perception of what their role in the stepfamily will be and their perceptions of what the roles of the other family members will be. Many problems can be traced to an important oversight: No one sat down with the others to define and clarify roles. They did not discuss thoroughly how all of them were going to fit together as a family. Many blended families find they lack the necessary communication tools to accomplish such a clarification of roles. Other parents, stepparents, children, and stepchildren discover to their dismay that they lack the necessary planning skills crucial to the successful blend of two families.

Subsequent chapters will discuss these four issues at greater length.

I
The Family

One of the underlying problems for stepfamilies is the task of blending family perceptions. Not only must stepfamilies blend two actual families—adults, children, homes, life-styles, goals, etc.—but they must also mentally blend their ideas of what "family" is all about.

Family Perception

A person forms a perception of what "family" is all about as a young child. This family perception is based on the family system modeled by the child's parents. The child learns what a family is, how parents behave, how children behave, what the rules are for family. When the child grows up, he or she marries and has this perception already set of what his or her own family should be like.

There is obviously a time gap between the child's formation of family perception and the adult's formation of an actual nuclear family. During these years, society has undergone a considerable amount of change. Things are different. Usually the person's idea of what "family" is all about also changes to accommodate the changed aspects of the surrounding world.

Family Styles

This process is considerably complicated by the fact that there are two basic family styles: the traditional family and the modern family. The child may grow up in a traditional family and form a traditional family perception; or the child may be raised in a modern family and adopt a more modern family perception. Of course, family styles vary considerably from culture to culture. This discussion of family styles is limited to a Western concept of family. A reader from an Asian, Latin, African, or other culture would, conceivably, focus on family styles, past and present, in their own culture.

The traditional Western family in its most traditional form looked something like this: It was headed by a patriarch and often included several generations. Extended family members lived nearby and were actively involved in family matters. Lines were clearly drawn between male and female roles. The father was in charge of the sons, with help from grandfather and uncles. The mother was in charge of the daughters, with help from grandmother and aunts. Father supported the family by working long hours. Frequently, though not always, mother was home full time with the children. Both parents felt a sense of duty toward the children and emphasized giving the children a "better life" than they, the parents, had. Their social life centered around family activities. They fostered a feeling of family closeness versus the world outside. They frequently treasured an ethnic background and taught their children to value this ethnic identity.

The diagram on page 11 illustrates this sequence in the following manner: At the top of the diagram (A) exist two family styles. The grandparents on the left lived a traditional family life-style. They raised their children to value this traditional life-style. A child from this family system grew up, married another traditional person, and together they set up a traditional family system for their child (circle). A period of time passes as the child grows up. The young adult meets a young adult from another family system (BB). They marry and are faced with the task of blending family perceptions because each has been raised in an opposite-style family system from

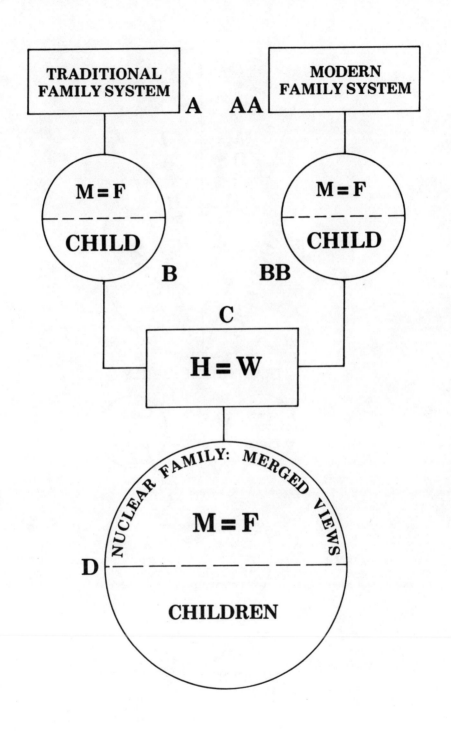

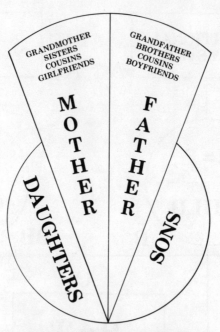

TRADITIONAL FAMILY

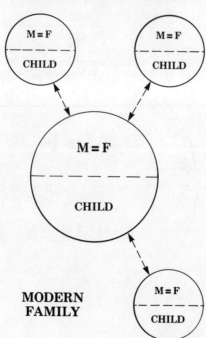

MODERN FAMILY

the other. The second young adult was raised to value a modern family system (BB), which originated in family system (AA) some years ago. So, husband and wife must reach a smooth blend of both family styles to coexist comfortably as the nuclear family (D). This is why few families are on the extreme end of the continuum. There are too many opportunities over generations for families to change to meet the changes in society.

The modern family looks something like this: Mother, father, and children form a nuclear family unit with loose ties to extended family members. Grandparents and relatives do not play an active role in the family. The nuclear family has, instead, ties to other similar nuclear families. These ties are called psychosocial kinships and provide moral support and social contact for the families involved. Both parents usually work outside the home and, together, share the task of raising the children, regardless of the sex of the children. Roles are not as clearly defined along male/female differences. Parents usually have more outside interests that do not center around the children. There is not a sharply drawn boundary between the family versus the outside world.

Of course, life is not this black and white, and families are not purely traditional nor purely modern. One could, instead, think of a continuum with both family styles at either end and degrees of style in between.

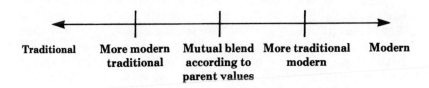

| Traditional | More modern traditional | Mutual blend according to parent values | More traditional modern | Modern |

CONTINUUM OF FAMILY STYLES

Family Perceptions in the Stepfamily

When two people marry, they must blend their ideas of what "family" is all about. This task is much more difficult if husband and wife were raised in opposite-style family systems. They will have conflicting ideas on relatives, roles, parenting, and work.

In the natural family, the spouses have time—time to blend these perceptions by dealing with these conflicts. The result is usually a family style somewhere on the continuum between traditional and modern.

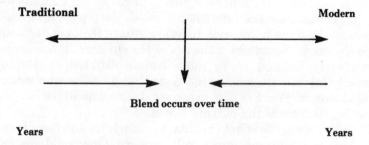

The stepfamily encounters two problems in this area of family perception. Husband and wife lack time to blend their perceptions, and they must also deal with *three or more* previous family systems.

One or both spouses in a stepfamily has been married before. The previously married spouse had a childhood perception of family, a perception as it was blended with the ex-spouse, and a perception of family as it was in the single-parent family system. The second or third family system was the model for the children of that marriage. If both spouses in the stepfamily have been married before, then they are faced with the difficult task of blending four to six perceptions of family. (See illustration on page 15.)

The problem occurs when parent and stepparent do not discuss their ideas on what a family should be and fail to share

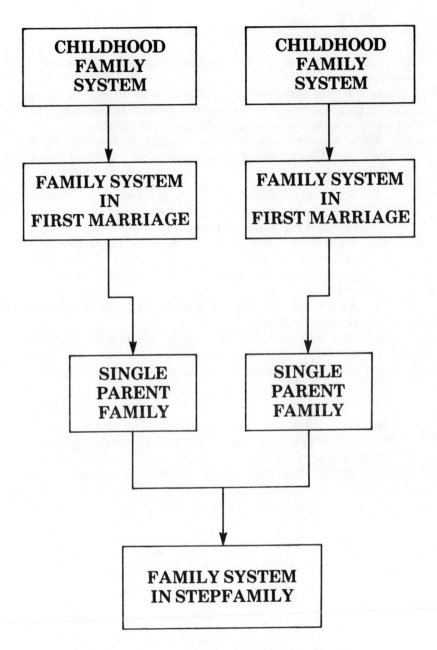

BLENDING FAMILY PERCEPTIONS

the past history of family systems. Each has a different perception of family, yet each partner *assumes* that the other spouse has the same values and beliefs as to how a family should be structured. These assumptions only come to light when conflict arises over what "family" is all about.

There are some simple steps to assist the new spouses in their efforts to blend family perceptions. Both spouses should discuss together:

1. What was your childhood perception of family? Describe the type of family system that your parents modeled for you as a child.
2. What type of family system or style did you and your ex-spouse create? Describe your ex-spouse's childhood perception of family and discuss the resultant merger of family styles.
3. As a single parent, did your ideas of what a family should be change?
4. How will your idea of "family" blend with your new spouse's perception of family? Are they similar? Very different? If different, what are the areas of compromise?

Any discussion will inevitably focus also on values—what is important and what is not important. The modern family style tends to emphasize a different set of values than does the traditional family. An effective blend of family perceptions will necessarily include a blending of values.

II
The Interim Period

The interim period follows a divorce or the death of a partner or parent. It is a transitional period of adjustment during which family members learn to become accustomed to the recent changes in the family system. It's important to note that *all* members—single parent, absentee parent, and children—experience this time of adjustment. Regardless of age, all members are affected by the breakup of the family.

The interim period may be preceded by divorce or death. Our first focus here will be on those families broken by divorce. The emotional scars of a divorce may be deep and long-lasting. During the initial stages of the interim period, pain is at its worst. Yet, this pain can be the fire that forges the steel within a person, an opportunity to strengthen one's inner resolve to build a new life.

Growth

The interim period for the adult can be an excellent opportunity for personal growth and development. As the pain decreases with time and as the anesthetic of the immediate survival problems wears off, the single parent can choose to capitalize on lessons learned from the divorce, such as relying on oneself—believing in one's ability not only to survive but also to cope successfully with life's ups and downs. The confident individual can seize the opportunity during the interim period to improve physical appearance and mental outlook. It can be a time to develop new skills, acquire new friends and interests, and find new or renewed satisfaction in work.

Mary, a thirty-two-year-old teacher, has two children who are ten and eight years old. She divorced her husband six years ago.

"When Bob and I first split up, I was panicky and afraid. I thought, 'My God, what am I going to do? How will we survive?' After a few weeks of self-pity, I decided that my life wasn't ending, it was just beginning! I'd been working as a teacher's aide for several years, and I felt I had some talent in this direction. I enrolled in a nearby college (I only had two years left to finish my degree) and found that the college has a Women's Center to help women like me. I was able to attend classes in the morning while the children were in school, and I continued to work afternoons as a teacher's aide. It wasn't easy, but we made it; the Women's Center really helped. The people there provided a lot of support and encouraged me to stick it out all the way to my teaching credential. It gave me confidence to know that others had been in my same situation and made it. Now I have a job that I enjoy and which allows me to spend evenings, holidays, and summers with my children."

Stagnation

The interim period may also provide the individual with an unfortunate opportunity for stagnation. It can be a chance to withdraw, wallow in self-pity, convince oneself of failure, and despair of any future successes. Ironically, an individual can find this withdrawal to be very "comfortable"— rationalizing feelings of insecurity by labeling them "self-sacrifice."

Bill, a twenty-nine-year-old bank officer, has had custody of his small son and daughter since his wife left him three years ago. He has a good job, a comfortable house, and security ... and has stagnated for the past three years. Since his divorce, Bill has refused to risk any new relationships. He has convinced himself that he is "not interested." When asked by his friends why he's not going out, he says, "I'm too busy with my work and with my family." Bill professes to be satisfied with his secluded life-style—denying any unhappiness, loneliness, or boredom. Bill's underlying feeling is one of anger and frustration because his wife left him and their children. He blames her for breaking up the family. In Bill's case, these feelings generalize to include all women.

This cycle of stagnation was broken through the efforts of Bill's best friend. He had been urging Bill to see a counselor for months and finally succeeded in getting Bill to agree to at least one visit. Once Bill had made this initial acknowledgment of a possible problem, he was able to progress to the acknowledgment of the reality of stagnation. Through counseling, Bill was able to make the transition to a healthier life-style, one in which he was willing to risk other relationships besides family and work.

The stagnating individual usually is unable to structure a truly healthy single-parent family because his or her focus is constantly on the negative aspects of life as a single parent. Therefore, it is essential for this individual to become involved in counseling to both assess and cope with these problems that will later lead to the establishment of an effective single-parent family.

The single parent who is experiencing growth, however, is often able to set up a healthy single-parent family because his or her focus is on the positive. One of the reasons that this may be so is simple: When a single parent is happy with his or her personal life and relationships, the single parent is a happier, more effective parent.

The Child's Interim Period

While adults can seek professional help during their

adjustment to the interim period (or talk to friends or find temporary relief at the corner bar), most children do not have the opportunity to seek professional help. They must rely on parents or close relatives for help in easing their adjustment to the interim period.

Parents can help children cope with divorce by accepting full responsibility for the divorce. Since children often have been used as the battleground for their parents' marital conflicts, they need to be reassured that they are *blameless*. They need to know that they are not at fault. The breakup of a family is difficult enough for the children; they do not need to experience additional grief or pain because of guilt.

Children during the interim period ask, "What happened?" Unfortunately, since children don't have the same opportunities to seek help that parents have and since parents are often preoccupied with their own pain of divorce, this question may remain unanswered. (Many still ponder the breakup of their family years later—as adults.) Confused, the children may arrive at the conclusion that the divorce was their fault, but keep this conclusion to themselves. Too often, parents fool themselves by thinking that their children are not affected by the changes... "they'll grow out of the confusion." True, they will grow physically, but they may remain confused emotionally.

Parents have a responsibility to help their children in the *present* by working through the questions and answers concerning divorce with their children. Without parental help and guidance, a child may harbor unrealistic beliefs in addition to feeling responsible for the divorce. The young child may fear being left alone, abandoned; he or she may feel very angry with one parent, especially the one who "left." Young children need the constant, stable structure of family life that they knew before the divorce. They need to be reassured that there is a place for them in both parents' new lives and that they will not be left out. Young children need to know that their parents intend to care for their needs and that their parents will still love them.

One young, single parent dealt with her little girl's need for reassurance in the following way:

"My little girl, Jennifer, walked around with a

worried expression on her face for days after I put our house up for sale. It was too big and expensive for the two of us and too time-consuming to take care of now that I had to do everything by myself. I thought I had explained all this to her pretty well and was involving her in the search for an apartment. What I didn't realize was that Jenny was too young to understand distance. She was worried that moving to a new apartment meant going to a new school and losing all her old friends! Boy, was I relieved when she finally confided her worries to me. I explained that we were only looking at apartments close enough so that she could go to the same school and see her same friends. She sat right up and smiled a beautiful smile of relief."

Older children, especially teens, may need this assurance and reassurance also. They need to know where they stand, what plans have been made for them in the changed family system, and what financial changes will affect them. They need to be made aware of what possible sources of professional help may be available, such as a school counselor, a teen drop-in center, or a professional youth service center.

Many parents choose to notify their child or teen's school principal, counselor, or teachers of the divorce. Often children and adolescents begin having trouble with teachers or peers in school; acting-out behavior is one method of trying to deal with confusion. Misbehavior or sudden academic problems may be a signal to parents. The child's behavior says, "Help! I don't understand." The solution is twofold. One, the parents need to help the child cope by frequent discussion and support. Two, if the school knows the child's home situation in these cases, school personnel will have a better grasp of the cause of the misbehavior and react with flexibility and understanding rather than rigidity and punishment. The child can be assisted in the adjustment and transition in a variety of ways. The school counselor may choose to talk individually with the child and encourage him or her to explore feelings about the divorce. Or, the school may choose to involve a group of such children in a counseling group specifically concerned with parental divorce.

A comfortable period of adjustment in which individuals

learn and grow—successful passage through the transitional interim period—is crucial to any future relationship whether it be a single-parent family or a stepfamily. The individual who (1) realizes that merely ending the marriage does not end all troubles, and (2) recognizes and honestly deals with the feelings caused by divorce and the fears of the unknown future, is on his or her way to successfully ending the interim period.

Death of a Parent

Although most individuals become single parents through divorce, a significant number of single parents have experienced the death of their spouse. In these cases, there is an added dimension to the interim period for both single parent and children—dealing with the death of the spouse or parent.

Elisabeth Kubler-Ross is an authority on death and dying. In her work with individuals and families, she has delineated several of the major issues involved in terminal illness and its effect on family members, especially the children. Kubler-Ross feels that most parents are not really prepared to help their children deal with the premature death of a young parent, and few of these youngsters are involved in professional counseling before, during, or after the parent's terminal illness. The result, Kubler-Ross has found, has been an increasing number of children who have repressed their early unresolved grief, are fearful of death, and avoid discussion of these issues. This can create problems in a future stepfamily.

Children will react in their individual characteristic ways to the death of a parent. Some children seem indifferent and continue with their activities as if nothing has happened. Other children choose to act out, become chronically truant, misbehave in inappropriate ways at home or school. Others may engage in promiscuous or delinquent behavior, or act defiant and provocative at a time when the surviving parent is least likely to notice due to his or her own grief and concentration on adjustment to the loss.

Yet, many children will behave in an opposite manner to these negative coping behaviors by becoming "too good." These children do all that is expected perfectly and "grow up overnight." Kubler-Ross believes that these young children who behave in this "too good" manner need a great deal of help, since they believe that death is temporary and that their good deeds will bring the dead parent back. Many harbor the belief that their "angry wishes" may have somehow been responsible for the parent's death.

Kubler-Ross concludes that parents need professional help with children who were deprived of sharing the dying process with the surviving parent and with children who show no signs of grief.

The Long-Dead Parent

In a future chapter on the Family Diagram, the issue of the long-deceased parent will be discussed. A few words at this point would be helpful in our discussion of the interim period.

During the interim period, it is crucial that professional help be sought to resolve the issues of the death of the parent. If this is not possible, then the family—surviving parent and children—needs to be able to discuss the dead parent and share the positive memories that parent left behind. Otherwise, the dead parent becomes a family ghost, someone never discussed but always present. This creates an unrealistic and problematic concern for the natural parent and future stepparent. The dead parent becomes saintlike—idealized in memory by the children as the perfect parent who never said a harsh word, never denied them anything, and never made a mistake. This "saint"—always there but rarely discussed freely with reminiscence about good qualities and faults—can be pretty hard to live with.

Whenever possible, the surviving parent should try to discuss and remember the deceased parent in a natural, warm, but realistic manner with the children. To fail to do so can create future problems similar to the following case.

Beth was thirteen years old when her father and stepmother brought her to a professional family counselor for help. Her parents had recently told Beth that her "mother" was actually her stepmother; her real mother had died when Beth was one and one-half years old, and her father had remarried one year later.

Beth's father had been reluctant to tell Beth the truth but had done so at the urging of relatives who feared that Beth would eventually find out from outside sources. Now Beth was acting moody and withdrawn, retreating to her room to listen to music for hours.

During the treatment, Beth revealed that she had always suspected the truth anyway, citing such clues as different physical appearances, the age gap between herself and her sisters, the absence of any baby pictures for her despite her sisters' full books, and certain comments unknowingly overheard over the years.

"What really bothers me is that neither of them will talk to me about my real mom. I need to know what she looked like. What was she like? Am I like her? How did she die?"

Beth wanted information, answers to all the hundreds of questions crowding her but didn't know how to ask. She sensed a reluctance to discuss the subject on her father's part—a vagueness surrounding the entire situation. Beth's father felt totally helpless to deal with Beth's questions. His first wife's death—a suicide—was still too painful to him, he felt, to discuss. Yet he understood his daughter's need to know. The compromise he arranged was to enlist the help of his mother who had known her first daughter-in-law since she was a young girl Beth's age. Grandmother and granddaughter spent several weekends together in which grandmother shared all her memories of Beth's mother, focusing on positive, shared qualities and answering all Beth's questions. She gave Beth the gift of many pictures of Beth's real mother, including several of mother and infant. After the initial ice was broken, Beth and her father were able to discuss the circumstances of Beth's mother's death; and, finally, father, daughter, and "mother" were able to discuss the present and pick up the pieces of their normal family life together.

III
Single-Parent Family

The result of every divorce that involves children is the creation of a single-parent family and an absentee-parent family. These new single-parent family systems may be brief or long-lasting.

The single parent has two responsibilities. He or she has a responsibility to self: to adjust to the divorce or bereavement by assuming the challenge of developing and growing as a person. He or she has a responsibility to the children: to restructure the family system by assuming the major responsibility for raising the children.

While juggling time for both of these tasks, the single parent often contends with both wanted and unwanted intrusions into the family circle from family, friends, and acquaintances. The single parent faces a reduced financial income and often has to relocate. Demands on time from career and family are increased.

The Single-Parent Mother

Although fathers are gaining custody with increasing frequency, in most divorce cases the mother becomes head of

25

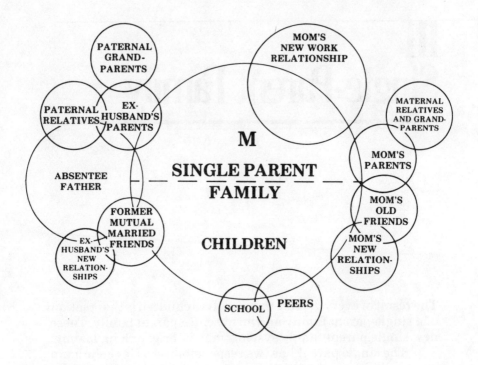

**Example
Single Parent Mother**

the new single-parent household. She may ask herself questions like, "How am I going to parent alone?" and, "How will I handle everything all by myself—taking care of the children, working, keeping up the house?" For the traditional mother, these concerns may loom intimidatingly at first. For the working mother, who has already been juggling career and family, these concerns may seem less significant initially. She may already be knowledgeable about day care and time management. She has had practice at fulfilling several roles simultaneously.

The single-parent mother has lost the security of her partner. Decisions must be made alone. The reality of finances must be faced; in most cases, single-parent mothers must deal with a reduced income. Oftentimes, the working mother's income may be insufficient to support the family at the previous standard of living, despite the child support contributed by the absentee father. She may need to seek a higher-paying job. In situations where mother has always remained at home as a housewife, the financial burden may be especially heavy. Frequently, this single-parent mother has no currently marketable skills and must either accept a low-paying, entry-level job or seek job training.

There are an increasing number of training programs for women in such situations. Local colleges offer reentry assistance for women going back to school. The federal manpower programs offer training and many positions for unemployed people. The hardest step for the single-parent mother to take is seeking the information she needs to become involved in these programs.

The working, single mother lacks *time*. She must spend the majority of her time at work, away from the home and her children. For the single mother, this lack of time often brings forth feelings of guilt. Mom must not only struggle to maintain a previous standard of living, but also, by these very efforts, deprive her children of a precious part of growing up: time with a parent.

Sometimes, single-parent mothers may feel that their lives have drastically changed; increased responsibilities may feel like a heavy burden. The resentful, single-parent mother may try to strike back at her ex-spouse, who is seen as having a carefree, easy time. This revenge may take several forms. A common one is that the mother spends more and more of her free time away from home. Children are left in the care of a baby-sitter or relative. Older children (sometimes as young as eight or nine years old) are left alone. The sad result is a lack of structure within the family and no daily parental model.

The single-parent mother is now free to make dating a part of her social life. However, the number of eligible women is frequently greater than the number of eligible men—a situation that may be compounded by the lingering social pressure against women dating men younger than themselves. In an extension of this attitude, many men decline to date women in their own age group in preference of those who are younger, all of which may make it a little more difficult for the single-parent mother to establish new dating relationships. Dating also puts another demand on mother's time; she must juggle family, career, and a social life.

Family pressures may cause another change in the life-style of the single-parent mother. The absentee father, removed from the day-to-day reality of the single-parent family, may apply subtle pressures. He may imply that his ex-spouse isn't doing an adequate job of raising his children: too little time spent with the children, too much time spent "running around," unsuitable men influencing his children, working bad hours, and time "wasted" at school. The list can be endless.

The extended family can be oversolicitous, a subtle implication of mother's lack of capability. The traditional grandparents may apply pressure through statements like, "A good mother shouldn't divorce her children's father." "A good mother doesn't date." A "good daughter" who accepts these values can destroy any chance for a happy future.

The single-parent mother's first responsibility in her new situation is to structure the single-parent family system, placing herself at the head of the family and letting each child know where his or her place in the family lies. This usually means delegating increased responsibilities to all children, depending upon their age and capabilities. The children need to have their mother discuss any new rules or guidelines that the new family system requires.

This restructuring may not be possible if the single-parent mother has not successfully resolved the issues of the interim period. Counseling at this point is usually vital in assisting the single-parent (male or female) in resolving personal feelings relating to the divorce such as depression, anxiety, and inadequacy. When the individual learns through counseling to effectively cope with these interim period issues, the single-parent family structure will be more positively strengthened. Counseling, in most of these cases, strengthens the single parent's sense of self and increases his or her self-confidence in his or her ability to meet the challenges of life as a single individual once again.

The single-parent mother must learn through counseling, reading, or the example of others to manage her *time*. Time is at a premium for the single-parent mother. She must budget time for self, for children—both as a group and individually, for family, for work, for dating, and for home. The process will not be easy and will probably take several months of trial and error to adequately achieve a balance comfortable for all involved.

The financial aspect of life for the single-parent mother can be more complicated. Budgeting time involves only the single parent and her children. Budgeting money, however, involves the absentee parent also. The single-parent mother must be willing to insist upon receiving, regularly, the child support due for her children. Since child support is awarded to secure the welfare of the children, the single-parent mother must be willing to press charges against the absentee parent if he fails to uphold the court agreement. Many single-parent mothers complain that their ex-spouse is irregular in his payments or has left the state and has not been heard from. Yet these mothers often drop the issue, saying nothing can be done. Many states, however, have legal agreements to assist the process of continued child support. Consulting a lawyer is a necessary step to ensuring delinquent child support payments.

Instruction in budgeting and managing the income from a job, child support, or any other source such as educational grants or loans, can be found in a number of places. Adult education at the local high school or community college often includes courses in personal finance. These courses can be very helpful.

Dealing with the pressure from an ex-spouse and extended family is a task that single-parent mothers must face alone or with the assistance of a counselor. Pressure from these sources usually makes the single-parent mother feel guilty. If she wants to resolve the guilt, the single-parent mother must satisfactorily answer the following questions: "Do your children have enough to eat? Do they have enough clothes? Do they have a comfortable place to live? Do they go to school? Are they doing well in school? Are you doing your best as a parent?" If the answer to all of these questions is yes, then the single-parent mother has no reason to feel guilty because of pressure from others.

As the single-parent mother learns to successfully balance family, work, and a social life, she will inevitably become involved in new friendships, perhaps new relationships. Some mothers handle dating and children effortlessly; others find themselves threatened by the competition and feel impelled to hide the fact that they have children. They fear their new relationships will not bear the strain.

For example, Sara, a thirty-five-year-old, single-parent mother had five children ranging in age from five to twelve. She had dated Bob for nine months; fearful of losing him, she had gone to elaborate lengths to hide the existence of her five children. She and Bob made plans to marry, he still ignorant of the situation and she anxious about the impending remarriage. Two weeks before their marriage, Bob got a surprise...

This story is intended to illustrate the absolute importance of honesty in any relationship. Sara's dishonesty severely shook the relationship when Bob learned the truth. He was not upset that Sara had five children; he was upset that she had not shared the existence of her family with him. The children felt a diminished sense of self-worth because they had to be hidden as if something was wrong with them.

A single-parent mother must work toward balancing both her needs and setting in proper perspective the responsibilities she has to her children. Once a healthy balance is found, the difficulties will not disappear but will become easier to deal with.

The Single-Parent Father

The end of the old relationship as husband marks the beginning of a new role for the single-parent father. His new role means new and difficult changes in his life. The single-parent father usually finds himself in the role of absentee parent (although, as mentioned, more and more fathers are gaining custody of the children). Whether the single-parent father has full- or part-time custody, he remains a parent with all the inherent responsibilities that parenting entails.

If a single-parent father has won full-time custody, he is charged with the responsibility of setting up a single-parent family structure with himself as the head of the family system and delegating responsibilities to the children according to their age and ability. He faces the same difficulties with custody as does the single-parent mother. He must juggle working, parenting, taking care of the home, and dating. These responsibilities make the same demands on his time and require time management in much the same manner as in the case of the single-parent mother.

The single-parent father must learn to budget his time for work and his time for the children. He may or may not be aware of a good day care center or a good baby-sitter. No longer can he automatically work late or leave for several days on business secure that his partner will care for the children in his absence. The security of parenting with a partner is gone.

If the full-time, single-parent father has previously left more of the household routine and daily child care to his wife, he may find himself unfamiliar with the sole responsibility for keeping his home running smoothly. He may feel pressure from his ex-wife or extended family to do a good job.

One advantage the single-parent father has over the single-parent mother may be his financial situation. The fact is that, typically, a man earns more than a woman. This higher income may mean that the single-parent father may find it easier to support his family than does the single-parent mother. However, it is by no means always true. Many single-parent fathers may sorely miss the income that their working wife contributed to the family. In these cases, it is just as crucial for single-parent fathers to insist on regular child support as it is for single-parent mothers. Otherwise, the burden of family support, house payments, day care, and all the other expenses associated with supporting a family may prove to be too heavy for his sole salary to bear.

Single-parent fathers may find it just as difficult as

single-parent mothers to handle dating. Balancing family life and responsibilities as a parent with social life and responsibilities to self may be extremely difficult.

Ed is a forty-five-year-old construction supervisor, a widower with custody of a ten-year-old daughter and fifteen-year-old son. He has been dating Alice, a forty-two-year-old woman whose children by a previous marriage are grown and living on their own.

"I asked Alice to marry me last month, but she hasn't been able to give me a definite yes or no yet. She says that she loves me but that she doesn't want to raise someone else's children at this point in her life. So right now, we're just taking it one day at a time. I don't know how we'll be able to resolve this. I love my two kids... maybe she'll learn to love them too."

Ed solved his dilemma for the moment by believing optimistically that Alice would change. She did not, and eventually they parted.

The single-parent father must face his family situation realistically. If his income is not sufficient to bear the responsibility alone (and even if it is, perhaps), then he must have no qualms about pressing for child support if his ex-wife becomes delinquent in her payments. If he is having difficulty parenting by himself or is unsure in his role of increased responsibility, help in the form of professional counseling is available; and he should not hesitate to seek it. There are also many excellent books on parenting, and local colleges offer parenting classes to the community. Counseling may be useful in assisting the single-parent father in dealing with any unresolved issues from the interim period.

The Absentee Parent

In most cases, the father's role after divorce is that of the absentee parent. In the event that the father gets custody of the children, the mother becomes the absentee parent. Whether mother or father, the absentee parent must adjust to the difficult reality that he or she will play a diminished role in the children's lives. Many absentee parents find this diminished role to be a constant source of agony and frustration. The day-to-day closeness is difficult to maintain and often compels the absentee parent to go overboard in his or her attempts to do it. These efforts often unintentionally sabotage the family structure that the single parent with custody is trying to establish.

Absentee parents often feel powerless to deal with the children's frustration over not being able to spend more time together with the non-custodial parent. It is difficult to help the children understand why the absentee parent left; they often feel shortchanged in that they no longer have daily access to both parents.

Some absentee fathers find it necessary to resolve some particularly difficult emotional issues. For example, if his spouse initiated the divorce, the father may find it difficult to sever emotional ties to his ex-wife. He may feel rage that his wife's action deprived him not only of her but also of his children. He may feel resentful and jealously brood over any new relationships between his ex-wife and other men. He may question his children about their mother's activities; his questioning places the children squarely in the middle of continuing conflict between their parents. Some children may prefer to see their father less rather than endure the questioning and subtle insinuations about their mother, or some will encourage discord to be the center of attention.

The absentee parent loses the security of the family system that was developed with much time and energy over the years. He or she frequently will not admit having felt comfortable within the security of the family circle. The absentee parent may find being alone far lonelier and far more risky than originally anticipated.

The demands on the middle-aged absentee father who is also experiencing a midlife crisis complicate his role. The midlife male may buy new "with it" clothes, a red sports car, and try to be a pal to his teen-age children rather than a father. His efforts to be a pal rather than a father places all of the burden of parenting on his ex-wife. Time with father becomes "fun time" where anything goes.

Absentee Parents' Dilemma

The dilemma of absentee parents—their diminished role in their children's lives—cannot be overstated.

First and foremost, absentee parents are reduced to onlookers in their children's day-to-day growing up. They are visiting parents in and out of the children's lives. The difficulties involved in maintaining regularly scheduled visits can be a constant aggravation. Visits are usually somewhat brief, somewhat planned, and, therefore, lack spontaneity and continuity. Activities tend to be centered around *entertaining* rather than sharing experiences as parents and children. Because time together is so limited, absentee parents may give in to the temptation to ignore misbehavior and choose *not* to parent or discipline. These actions are based on a desire to make time together "special"—to make up for all the lost time between visits.

Usually, but not always, guilt is an underlying motive behind most absentee parents' behavior. They must deal with their guilt over leaving the family, guilt over not playing a major role in raising their children, and guilt over their well-intentioned but nonetheless harmful shirking of parenting while visiting with the children.

Two common mechanisms employed by absentee parents in this position are suppression and projection. They may deny that they feel any guilt whatsoever and, instead, focus on the "poor job" the ex-spouse is doing raising the children. These defense mechanisms protect their own egos but prevent absentee parents from successfully adjusting to their role in the family system.

Joint Custody

A few words on the issue of joint custody should be said here. Joint custody describes the situation in which both parents agree to share custody of the children. They divide the children's time equally, consult on major decisions, and parent the children equally.

The objections to joint custody revolve around three issues. One, many people believe that children are better off with their mother. Two, two people who divorce in conflict will be unlikely to maintain an amiable and equal partnership in parenting. Three, the child in joint custody is continually uprooted, lacks a feeling of continuity and stability, and feels physically and emotionally split in half.

In a study of forty couples practicing joint custody, Mel Roman of the Albert Einstein College of Medicine found that joint custody is working for all of them. The children are thriving and the parents are themselves working out new and productive life-styles. He found that parents involved in joint custody shared an ability to isolate their marital difficulties from their parental duties. Two additional ingredients important to the success of the arrangement are geographical closeness and some degree of communication between the parents.

More research remains to be done in the area of joint custody before any firm conclusions can be made concerning the advantages or disadvantages and benefits or harm of such a custody arrangement. We can conclude, however, that joint custody avoids the bloodshed of a custody battle.

Children in a Divorce

Too often parents feel that divorce will permanently harm the children. They stay together for the "children's sake." The reality is that children are harmed far more by growing up in a two-parent family system of discord and conflict than by growing up in a single-parent family system that is nurturing and supportive.

Children need help during this crucial time in their young lives. This help must come from important adults in their lives. An often-repeated myth is that children grow out of it or have an easy time dealing with change because they are kids. This is not true. Children need help and frequently do not receive it.

Preceding and following the breakup of the family, parents and children are in a state of crisis. Mother and father may seek help by entering therapy, by talking to friends, by reading self-help books, or by escaping through drugs or alcohol. The children do not have these tools at their disposal. They are unfamiliar with outside sources of aid; they've always sought help from within their family. Their family has been their world. They can't arrive at any answers because they often don't understand the questions.

They find themselves powerless against embarrassment about their parents' divorce, anger at one parent's departure, confusion concerning the changes, and fear about the future. Children express these feelings in a variety of ways: acting out at home or in the classroom, denying that the divorce is real, withdrawing from the situation, or becoming ill.

The Big Issue: Blame

Most children will seek someone to blame for the divorce and disruption of the family. They may expend a great deal of energy first blaming one parent, then blaming the other parent. In most cases, they eventually settle the blame on themselves.

If he or she were a better child, better son or daughter, better student...if he or she had only tried harder...then mother and father would not have divorced. This silent blaming of themselves often goes unnoticed for several weeks, months, or even years.

One counselor asked a group of thirty junior high students whose parents were divorced the following questions. "How many of you think your mother is to blame for the divorce?" None of them raised their hand. "How many of you think your father is to blame for the divorce?" Two hands waved in the air. "How many of you think that you are to blame for your parents' divorce?" Twenty-eight hands shot up in the air.

The counselor spent the next hour with the students working through this guilt. Since most children see events egocentrically, many of the students had been unable to see the dynamics of the divorce. Mother and father have three major roles: self, husband or wife, and parent. The counselor drew the following diagram and pointed out the crucial fact that husband and wife divorce, *not* mother and father.

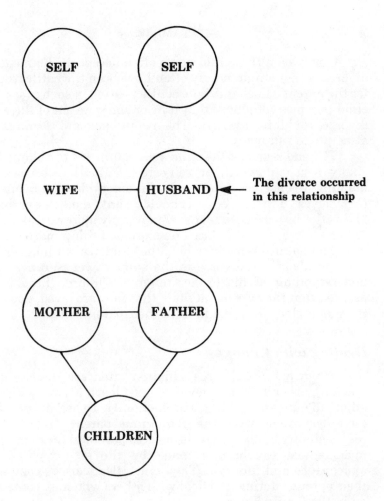

The divorce occurred in this relationship

Children can cause problems in *families*, between mother and father and children. They are not the cause of problems in the husband and wife relationship; that should be separate from the parent/child relationship. If parents divorce, it is because they no longer can live together as husband and wife. Parents remain parents; they do not divorce their children. The relief in the room could be felt. Many of these children had carried around the feeling of being responsible for the divorce for years.

One reason that children so often accept the blame for a divorce is that children may often have been the battleground for the parent's husband/wife conflict. Often in such cases, the child becomes convinced that if he or she were out of the way, divorce could be averted. The result: suicidal feelings or attempts to run away.

The end result of the child's acceptance of the blame is a shaky sense of worth or self-esteem. Months or years of blaming themselves has meant innumerable statements to themselves, "I'm no good," "I shouldn't have done this or that," "I'd better be perfect so I'll never make any more mistakes," or "I'm hopeless, so what does one more bad thing matter..."

The natural remedy to help the child deal with his or her feelings about the divorce is the support, reassurance, and understanding of his or her parents. Children need to be assured that they are not at fault, that they are loved, and that there is a place for them in both their parents' lives.

Dealing with Changes

When parents divorce, children often see the world as cracking around them. They now must learn to cope with and adjust to numerous changes in the family. To begin with, they have less time with the remaining parent, have added responsibility because there is one less parent in the home, and must adjust to changes made by the single parent in appearance and life-style. They must also learn to cope with their parents' dating and deal with others who may come and go in the family home.

One important help for children is learning to get out of the middle when caught between parents who are still in conflict.

Billy returns home after spending the weekend with his father...

MOM: Hi, Billy! Did you have a nice time?
BILLY: Yeah, it was O.K.
MOM: Did your father have anyone else over visiting?
BILLY: Yes, his girfriend was there.

MOM: I guess it wasn't much fun for you with her there.
BILLY: Oh, it was O.K. I had a good time.
MOM: If your Dad really cared about you, he wouldn't
         have her there when you visit.
BILLY: Oh.

In this situation, Billy's mother puts him in the middle where he doesn't belong and feels uncomfortable. Children should make a bargain with each parent, if necessary, not to be asked about the activities of the other parent during the time of their visit. This way, the child is more likely to look forward to visiting and less likely to be caught in the cross fire that often exists between divorced parents with unresolved problems. Often a teacher, counselor, or relative can be instrumental in helping the child learn to bargain. For example, the school counselor could coach the child on how to approach the parents and ask them to allow him or her to get out of the middle.

Children may, as a defense against dealing with the changes, cling to the fantasy that "It's only temporary—my parents will get back together again." Parents must firmly but gently reinforce the permanency of the split and encourage the child to accept this reality.

Even unhappy marital ties don't break easily. Two adults may divorce as husband and wife, but they don't divorce as mother and father. The parent bond still links them for better or worse. Single parent may be dependent on absentee parent financially or in a time of crisis. Absentee parents still play an important role in the children's lives and need their ex-spouse's cooperation to fulfill their role. Both parents need to develop independent lives yet must maintain a good working relationship where their children are concerned.

This cooperation does not occur magically. Both single and absentee parents need to behave in a mature manner; personal resentments or jealousies must not be allowed to interfere with their role as parents.

Most children will not reach a comfortable adjustment to divorce and the single-parent family without the help of their parents. The ultimate outcome is the responsibility of those parents.

IV
Stepfamily Versus Original Family

Many people minimize the differences between the stepfamily and the original family. They enter the relationship confident that everything will work out because they want it to. When things don't automatically work out, spouses begin to have grave doubts about their chances for success in their remarriage. By expecting immediate success, they set themselves up for failure and the mind-set that stepfamilies don't work.

Stepfamilies can be successful. They can't be the same as the original family, and members should not try to mirror the previous family. It's important to note that stepfamilies can, in many cases, be *better* than the original family. They are generally more stable because spouses are more mature through the growth experience of their divorce and are willing to expend considerable positive energy to make this second marriage a success. This chapter will discuss the how of this relationship in greater detail.

Success in the steprelationship requires a great deal of time and energy. It requires honest communication, a willingness to define and clarify roles, and an ability to laugh at and learn from mistakes. Most of all, it requires both a desire to make it work and a willingness to put forth the necessary effort.

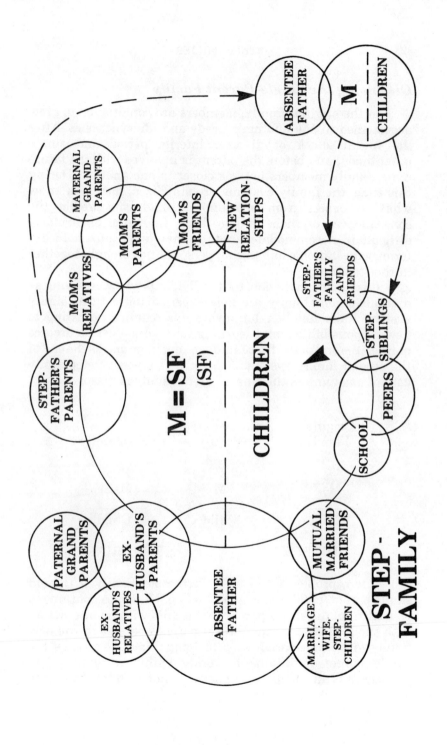

Dissolving the Single-Parent Family

In the original family, members are conditioned to grow accustomed to one another's needs and idiosyncrasies. After the initial shock of divorce, interim period and single parenthood, and before the parent is involved with the future mate, family members become closer to one another. During this time, the family customs are stabilized; members know what to expect from one another and can predict the consequences of their actions. It is, therefore, particularly difficult to accommodate another change—to adjust to differing expectations, habits, and personalities brought together in the stepfamily.

It is important to note that individuals who were living as a single-parent family are now experiencing a third family system. Each family relationship has required adjusting to new responsibilities and learning new roles. Just as divorce marked the end of the first family, remarriage marks the end of the second family system. A healthy, supportive stepfamily cannot exist unless the single-parent family is dissolved.

Original Family	Single-Parent Family	Stepfamily
	P	P=SP
M=F	M	M=SF
————	————	————
Child	Child	Child
DIVORCE		REMARRIAGE

Often, problems will arise in the stepfamily if the old single-parent/child bonds go unbroken. Messages continue to be sent from the single parent to the child with no interaction with the stepparent. The natural parent operates in the new family with single-parent ways of doing things. In essence, the single parent maintains a family within a family. The stepparent is an outsider—a spouse but not a parent. There has been little or no blending of ideas and individuals. The results are dissatisfying to everyone involved, but especially to the stepparent.

This failure to dissolve the single-parent family within the stepfamily has several sources. A great deal of effort and work went into establishing the single-parent family, which may have been in existence for years. It is, therefore, difficult to relinquish the hard-won, established way of living. Another factor involves the oldest child in the single-parent family. This child is often elevated to a sort of surrogate spouse or co-parent status and is in charge in the single parent's absence. When the parent remarries, it may be difficult for the teen-ager to abandon a long-standing role. This may result in conflict with the stepparent, jealousy, acting out, and a concerted effort to disrupt the new relationship. The natural parent may marry because he or she wants a mate, not necessarily because he or she wants another partner in parenting.

It is crucial for stepfamilies seeking answers to their problems to begin by exploring the possibility that this "family within a family" exists within their own stepfamily system. If this is the case, it is the responsibility of the former single parent to dissolve the old single-parent family system immediately. This can only be accomplished by open discussion and concerted effort by all. Failing to do so will prevent the necessary transition from single-parent family to stepfamily. The stepparent will continue to feel like an outsider in his or her home.

A note to remember: The ceremony that symbolized the remarriage did more than celebrate the union of two people and the creation of a stepfamily; it also marked the dissolution of the single-parent family system.

Expectations upon Becoming a Stepfamily

Problems may occur when members of the stepfamily enter the new venture with unrealistic expectations. It is important that stepfamily members discuss their expectations and explore together the reality or unreality of these expectations. Time and time again, when left unexplored, these

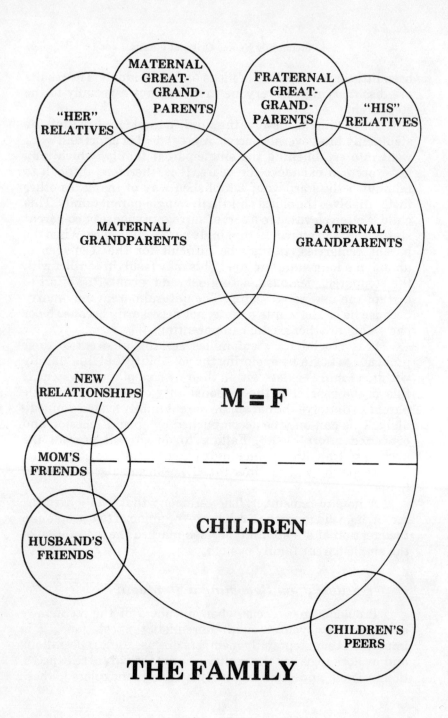

"HER" RELATIVES

MATERNAL GREAT-GRAND-PARENTS

FRATERNAL GREAT-GRAND-PARENTS

"HIS" RELATIVES

MATERNAL GRANDPARENTS

PATERNAL GRANDPARENTS

NEW RELATIONSHIPS

M = F

MOM'S FRIENDS

HUSBAND'S FRIENDS

CHILDREN

CHILDREN'S PEERS

THE FAMILY

unrealistic expectations slip out to trip up family relationships.

Children bring to the stepfamily a legacy of learning and experiences from the original family and from the interim period. Caution may be uppermost in their expectations— wanting to first find out what their relationship to this new person will be. Children are sometimes coached by parents to focus only on the positive aspects of their parents' remarriages and suffer a rude awakening to the reality of stepfamily life. On the other hand, children often pessimistically expect the worst from the new relationship and refuse to invest their emotions, focusing only on the negative aspects.

Parents' expectations are varied. They may expect magic from the second marriage. Having survived a difficult previous relationship and, perhaps, a tough period of single parenthood, some husbands and wives may count on the new marriage to solve all the old problems. They may even actively promote this expectation; to do otherwise might deter the prospective partner from the altar. Parents may assume that the stepfamily will function the same way as the original family, overlooking the fact that the very nature of the blended family makes this impossible.

Unrealistically, the soon-to-be-married parents may expect that each will love the other's children—*instantly*. Previously unmarried stepparents may expect to "just know how to parent"... how to deal with children. The natural parent may push the stepparent to immediately assume a parental role that was, perhaps, unfulfilled or lacking in the previous marriage or during the single-parent days.

Some stepparent candidates feel that the children are part of the package deal. Others expect that they will be able to make up to the stepchild any hurts or deprivation suffered prior to the remarriage. Some stepparents-to-be who have never been married nor had any children expect to receive benefits from joining a ready-made family, such as making up for all the family life they've missed.

We realize that it would be totally unrealistic to expect individuals to be unaffected by these expectations. Through open discussion, members of the future stepfamily can keep the expectations in the proper perspective.

Myths in the Stepfamily

The pervasive myths concerning the steprelationship are quite similar to expectations. Together, the two shade the color and quality of life in the stepfamily.

The most well known of the many myths are the "wicked stepparent" and "instant love." Members in a stepfamily cannot remain unaffected by these myths. By clarifying them, however, family members can put them into perspective. Family members can see them for what they are—fairy tales and make-believe.

The myths of the "ugly stepmother" or "cruel stepfather," for instance, are repeated over and over in fairy tales. Yet a fairy tale is just that—a fairy tale and nothing more. No woman is automatically a "wicked stepmother"; she may, however, choose to act like one. She may want to marry a man and convince him that she would love to parent his children. Once married, she may refuse to accept the responsibility of another woman's children. She may pit herself against the children and deal with them on an adult level. She may refuse to allow them to be children and blame them for her own unhappiness with the situation.

The stepmother must define her role and clarify how she intends to occupy her central position. She must decide whether or not she is willing to parent someone else's children. This must be done before she establishes herself as part of the family. Otherwise, it is likely that she will become miserable and create not only an "ugly stepmother" personality, but also an unhealthy family situation.

No man is automatically a "cruel stepfather"; he may, however, choose to act like one. He may marry a woman and convince her that he will be a strong yet loving father. Once married, his "strength" may be abusive and overwhelming. He may blame and deal harshly with the stepchildren for all transgressions.

The stepfather must also define his role and clarify how he intends to occupy his central position. He must decide to be a partner not a dictator. Otherwise, he will perpetuate the myth.

A stepparent must work with the help of his or her mate to

become a good, supportive parent. It is important for parents and children to realize that myths do exist. Understanding the dynamics of the myths greatly helps to put them in perspective.

Fortunately, the reality of having a stepparent is vastly different from the myth of having a stepparent. This myth should be exposed as presenting the rarity not the reality. Most stepparents accept a difficult role with willingness and a sincere desire to be an important and effectively positive part of the stepchildren's lives. They enter the relationship willing to give of themselves 100 percent in a difficult situation. They do *not* deserve to bear the brunt of these tasteless myths. The role of stepmother and stepfather will be discussed in the following chapters.

The second most commonly mentioned myth is that of "instant love." Soon-to-be stepparents often think, "I love you, I'll love your kids." Children may feel "I have to love this person—it's my stepparent," or "My new stepparent will love me, and treat me great." Parents might optimistically think, "My fiancée loves me . . . he or she will love my children as soon as we're all living together." The reality is that the real thing—living together as a family—is very different from living separately, relating to each other as parent's friend or fiancée's children. Obviously living together is very different from going on outings together to the park or movies.

"Instant love" does not exist. Love takes time to develop and grow between people. But love in the stepfamily is not a requirement of happiness in the stepfamily. Mutual respect and consideration between stepparent and stepchild can be a positive ingredient to success.

Time in the Stepfamily

One obvious difference between the original family and the stepfamily is the element of *time*. In the original family, a couple courts each other one to one, decides to marry, and marries. The couple then has a period of time as husband and wife, ranging from months to years, in which to adjust to living together, to blend life-styles, define roles, and to discover one another's idiosyncrasies. In short, they have the time and opportunity to cement their couple bond, their relationship as husband and wife. Together, they plan the expansion of their family; they plan the first child and subsequent children and have months to prepare for parenthood. As the family grows, the couple and children have time to adjust to living together. As the years pass, they share a common family history.

Of course, this is the ideal progression of events in a family's formation. Many families do not have the luxury of this orderly progression. For example, a wife may be pregnant at the time of the marriage or the couple may live together yet fail to develop a true closeness or cememt their sense of "we."

The stepfamily lacks the crucial element of time. Frequently, the courtship takes place around the children. There is no time between marriage vows and parenthood to cement the couple bond—it's an instant family. Family members do not share a common history and they bring very different legacies to the steprelationship. In the confusion of "instant family," members may neglect to clarify and define roles. Their differences are new to one another and often cause friction among them.

This element of time gains perspective when one considers the planning involved in an adoptive family. The adoptive couple applies to adopt a child and usually endures a long waiting period. During this period of time, the adoption agency carefully screens the couple. The prospective parents must prove that they both sincerely desire a child, that they have a marriage of proven stability, and that they can provide a good home. In a stepfamily, there are no safeguards to ensure that the stepparent wants a stepchild, or that the marriage will be stable and long-lasting, or that the new family will be financially secure.

Husband and wife in the stepfamily must give themselves the time together to cement their relationship as a married couple. This is difficult to do surrounded by the constant demands of children.

A Practical Suggestion

Husband and wife should "escape" at least every six weeks for a weekend alone. This time can be spent relaxing and getting to know one another, free from family pressures. Often stepparents protest that this retreat for privacy is impossible— no time, no baby-sitters, can't afford it. Spouses in a stepfamily can't afford not to. To neglect their relationship as husband and wife, to fail to cement that bond between them could destroy any chance for success in the steprelationship.

Changes

Other obvious differences involve the many changes experienced by stepfamily members.

Most stepfamilies usually juggle two last names. This can foster a feeling of separateness or not belonging. It can cause confusion at school, church, and with friends.

Birth order is not the constant it has always been. The oldest child may become a middle child...the youngest child may become an older child. One child may find himself sharing a classroom with a stepsibling. Another child may have to learn to help care for younger stepsiblings. Older children may find themselves adjusting to even older stepsiblings caring for them.

Most stepfamilies must also deal with the "revolving door": noncustody children come to visit, custody children leave to visit, mutual children stay put. Orchestrating visitation schedules can be a demanding task. Holidays, birthdays, and vacations can cause a headache to the parents trying to be considerate of everyone involved in the stepfamily.

In stepfamilies in which the natural parent is a widow or widower, there are not these revolving-door problems. However, the issue of death is a factor to be considered. Have the children (and their parent) successfully adjusted to the loss? Many stepchildren feel a taboo against talking about their dead parent, yet this very secrecy propagates the unresolved feelings. Parent and stepparent should actively work to remove any unspoken prohibitions against talking about the dead parent and former family system. This openness removes the mystery and makes a clear distinction between past and present.

Another change for members of the stepfamily concerns intrusion. The boundaries in the stepfamily are not as clearly drawn nor as equally respected by relatives and friends. There are too many people involved. The stepfamily encounters both well-intentioned and meddling intrusion from four sets of grandparents, four sets of relatives, the absentee parent, and numerous friends. One stepparent described this intrusion as "like living in a fishbowl."

This intrusion can take several forms. Consider the following example:

The Richardson family consists of Bob and Joan Richardson, his five grown children from a previous marriage, his daughter who is fifteen years old, her son who is sixteen years old, and her three grown children from a previous marriage. On Christmas Eve, the agreed-upon plan was for all the children to gather at the Richardsons' for an early evening buffet. Then Joan's children would leave to visit their father in a nearby city. On Christmas Day, all the children would join Bob and Joan and their surviving grandparents for a traditional Christmas dinner of turkey and all the trimmings.

Yet the plan failed, leaving Joan and Bob and the grandparents feeling disappointed and let down. The adult children all came at different times on Christmas Eve, which meant that everyone ate at different times. Then Joan's children drove the forty miles to see their father only to find that he was not at home. On Christmas Day, Joan's children received a call from their father, and anxious to see him, they left immediately after the meal to visit him. Joan, Bob, and the grandparents felt cheated out of a family gathering. Bob's children were left feeling somehow responsible for the unsettled atmosphere.

These changes point out the different demands on stepfamily members; the experience of living in step requires members to meet the challenge and work toward blending the family. The steps to meet this challenge will be discussed in a later chapter.

V
Defining Roles

Stepfamily...the very word brings to mind negative connotations. The term indicates the presence of a number of players not present in the original family. The major players in this family are the natural parent, stepparent, absentee parent, natural child, stepchild, siblings, stepsiblings, grandparents, and stepgrandparents. All of these people form a family system that has members both inside and outside of the immediate family circle. All of these people have a role: what they are in a situation, their actions, attitudes, beliefs, and behaviors.

All family members bring to the steprelationship their own individual perceptions of their role in the blended family and their individual perceptions of the roles of other members. Frequently, these role perceptions are not verbalized and shared. Each assumes the other members all think along the same lines.

In the blended family, the possibility for conflict can be enormous due to one important oversight: The members didn't sit down together to define and clarify roles.

The following discussions will focus on the roles of the unique individuals in the stepfamily. Stepmother, stepfather, absentee parent, stepchild, and natural parent...their separate roles and positions in the new family unit will be examined.

The Stepparent's Role

The role of a stepparent can be very complex because of the many variables involved. The role of stepparent—a man or woman previously unmarried who marries someone with children, or a man or woman who has children from a previous marriage and who marries someone with children from a previous marriage—is the focus of this chapter.

A man becomes more than a husband when he marries a woman with children; he becomes a stepfather. A woman becomes more than a wife when she marries a man with children; she becomes a stepmother.

Stepparents find themselves faced with some unsettling issues. They occupy a central position in the family—that of a parent—yet lack the power base of a natural parent. And how much of a parent is a stepparent? Where is the fine line between parenting and stepparenting?

Many stepparents may feel like intruders in someone else's home, or they may feel like they are intruders in their own home. Many stepparents may feel that the stepchildren don't really listen to them. Others feel as if they are in competition with the stepchildren's absentee parent or with the memory of the deceased natural parent. Some stepparents may not feel comfortable if they feel the responsibility for mothering or fathering falls exclusively to them as is sometimes the case when the natural parent has been long absent or deceased.

Some stepparents ask, "What am I supposed to do?" "What do I want to do?" "What role does my spouse expect me to take with the children?" "What is my spouse willing to allow me to do?" "How can we work together as husband/wife, parent/stepparent?"

From Spouse to Stepparent

Most prospective stepparents don't view the stepfamily in perspective. During courtship, the stepparent-to-be may have been "in control": setting the scene for becoming acquainted, establishing friendship, and participating in carefully structured family activities. After marriage, stepparents find themselves in day-to-day proximity to the children, no longer in control of setting the scene.

The transition from being single to mate to stepparent is usually marked by one of two expectations. One, the stepparents may feel that they instantly know just how to parent the children, thus becoming "superparent"; or, two, they'll stay in the background, pleading lack of knowledge, and leave the parenting to the natural parent, thus becoming a "reluctant stepparent."

SUPERDAD

John, a general sales manager of a large company, was a thirty-three-year-old husband who was excited over becoming a stepfather to three little girls. He just *knew*, with 100 percent confidence, that he was going to be good at parenting. He was confident that the girls would call him "Dad" right away. With supreme calm and confidence, John beamed his way through the wedding festivities. He efficiently supervised the preparations to leave on the honeymoon. He proudly ushered his new bride, new stepdaughters, and their large, shaggy dog into his compact car and set off on their "honeymoon" to another state.

"I got as far as Los Angeles before I realized I was in trouble, that maybe there were some things to parenting that I didn't know. We'd only been on the road one and one-half hours, and I'd heard, 'John, I have to go to the bathroom,' four separate times, and we'd made four separate stops. I really lost my cool."

John is an example of someone who was more than willing to parent, but was handicapped by a lack of knowledge. In his eagerness to be a father, he rushed into parenting (like the confident supervisor he was) by planning a family vacation rather than a honeymoon. In addition, he set himself up to fail by setting very high personal standards. He expected himself to win the girls' love immediately and to handle all situations expertly. Despite his inexperience, he did not allow for any mistakes.

In John's situation, he assumed that he would be a "perfect" stepfather, actually father, since he immediately wanted to act and be seen as the father in the family. He did not realize, as new stepparents new to parenting must realize, that he would need to proceed carefully. He would learn to parent one day, one week, one month at a time. He would make mistakes, but, with his wife's support, he could increase his successes in stepparenting as time went on by learning from his mistakes.

RELUCTANT PARENT

The reluctant stepparent is the spouse who, for various reasons, would prefer not to parent the children. One type of reluctant stepparent is the individual who has been previously married, has raised a family (the children are grown and on their own), and chooses to ignore the fact that the new mate has children.

The individual who marries despite his or her reluctance concerning stepparenting will encounter frustration. Merely ignoring the children will not change the situation; in most cases the natural parent will not give up custody of the children or visitation rights. The result is that often the natural parent will feel equally frustrated and caught in the middle between spouse and children.

Frank is a previously married forty-five-year-old educator and father of three grown children, all of whom are married. His second wife, Mary, is thirty years old and has a ten-year-old daughter. Mary would like Frank to be an active and interested stepfather, playing an important role in parenting her young daughter. Frank, however, wants nothing to do with more parenting. He wants to have more time with his wife to travel and lead a carefree existence. He is in rivalry with his young stepdaughter; he wants time alone with his wife, while his stepdaughter wants time with and attention from her mother.

Frank brought into his second marriage an expectation that he would have his new wife all to himself despite the obvious reality that she had a ten-year-old daughter. He chose to ignore the existence of the child during the courtship. Mary assumed that he would change once they were married. Frank denied the reality that a child requires time and parenting by two parents. He married regardless of the conflict between his desire for a full-time wife and her desire to share the parenting with a full-time stepfather. His reaction to the situation? He drew back, refusing to have anything to do with the child. He became a reluctant stepfather. After two years, the situation became untenable and they separated.

Jan, a forty-seven-year-old mother of three grown children, has been dating a forty-five-year-old father with custody of his two teen-agers. Robert has asked Jan to marry him several times.

"I love Robert very much and would love to be his wife. But I know it won't work. Robert has tried to convince me over and over that his children will not create any problems between us. He says that we'll all get along fine and that I really won't have to be their stepmother or anything. I know myself, though; and I just don't want to have to go through helping raise adolescents again. Those years with my own kids were the hardest years I've ever experienced, harder even than my divorce. Robert's ex-wife lives back East and has only seen them once in the last six years. I know that I'll be forced to parent, and I'm just not willing to. So, I've continued to see Robert, but I won't marry him. I don't know how long our relationship will continue with this stalemate."

In Jan's situation, she was able to recognize her reluctance to stepparent rather than ignore it. She chose to continue her relationship with Robert on her own terms. She realized that she would not be a good stepparent and wasn't willing to be convinced otherwise or change her belief. Reluctant stepparents must be willing to admit to their feelings prior to any remarriage. Failure to do so usually leads to future unhappiness and even divorce.

A second type of reluctant stepparent can be described as

follows. This individual usually professes a desire to form a
family and take an active role as a stepparent. He or she seems
pleased that the future spouse has children. Yet after the
marriage takes place, the stepparent seems to actively promote
the idea that the children would be better off living with the
absentee parent. It almost seems that the stepparent is trying
to get rid of the children.

This problem can only be avoided by honest consideration
of true feelings before the remarriage. It's a topic that parent
and stepparent must thoroughly discuss; to fail to do so is
irresponsible and can mean much heartache for parent,
stepparent, and children in the future.

Happily, most stepparents are not reluctant stepparents.
Most of them accept the challenge of helping to raise another's
children gracefully and become actively involved in parenting
in the stepfamily. Indeed, some stepparents consider it an
honor to be a stepparent. One divorced woman remarried a man
with two young children and one teen-ager. She shared her
feelings with a group of stepparents one evening:

> "I was really thrilled at the prospect of helping raise
> my husband's three children. I'd always wanted to
> have children but couldn't. This is the closest I'll ever
> be to a mother, so I'm really glad to be a stepmother. I
> find the rewards are tremendous, and my life is much
> richer now."

Establishing a Role

But what about those stepparents who do want to assume
the parenting role? They are not reluctant nor do they have the
unrealistic idea that they can be a superparent. The problem
then is one of establishing this parenting position or role. In so
doing, the previously unmarried person may be at a disadvantage; he or she may have no previous parenting experience.

Establishing a role may be simply asserting oneself in the
family. An unspoken assumption in stepfamily mythology is
that the stepparent's role is to play no role at all. Stepparents

have a role—*if they choose to define it*. In order to do so, they need the assistance and support of their spouse.

The rest of this chapter will focus on individual aspects of the stepparent's role. The diagram below presents these role characteristics graphically.

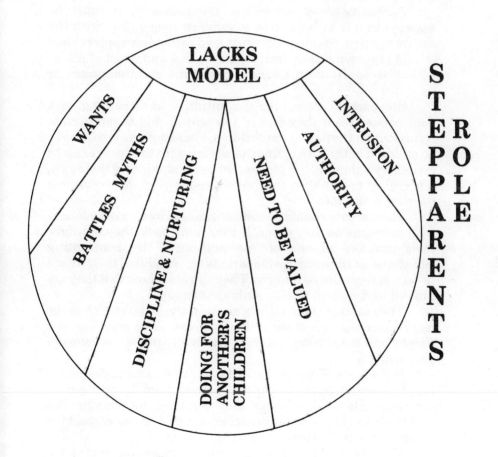

Authority

The starting point of a role definition for the stepparent is that the stepparent will function as the male or female head of the household. With the natural parent's cooperation, the stepparent must assert this position of authority, head of household, early in the steprelationship. If the stepparent tries to "wait for the right moment" in a few months—or years—it is likely that he or she will never effectively function comfortably as head of household.

Authority does not come automatically; it must be asserted in a firm consistent manner in cooperation with the natural parent. Stepparents must lead rather than order. They should state what they feel, offer opinions and, most of all, be willing to confront on issues of discipline and inappropriate behavior.

Stepparents must take the initiative in discussing with their spouse what they feel is appropriate and inappropriate behaviour on the part of the children. For stepparents who have no children of their own, this discussion with the spouse can be extremely valuable. For stepparents with children of their own, it is crucial to establish the guidelines for *all* of the children in the new household.

Stepparents should be confrontational by choosing to deal with problems as they occur. If they hang back, they reinforce their position as one of "no authority." By confronting situations as they occur, stepparents can establish their intent to take active roles as parents. They can also show that they are human and willing to risk making mistakes.

The children must clearly see that the stepparent has the respect and support of the natural parent. They must see that parent and stepparent act together as a team on decisions of parenting.

If the natural parent is still operating in a single-parent family, the stepparent cannot parent from a position of authority. He or she is excluded, kept on the outside. The children can clearly see this exclusion and will not respect the stepparent's authority as a parent.

Usually, what will happen in this situation is that the

stepparent will withdraw from asserting him or herself as a partner in heading up the household and move toward a more withdrawn position outside the family circle.

Intrusion

Individuals who previously led single lives often have no idea of what living with someone else's children will be like. They often discount the reality that there are children. They feel that children will be no problem once they are married. They predict that the children will interfere less with their lives—getting married means that they will have more time together as a couple. They focus more on their expectations as spouse than as stepparent.

The couple often promotes this focus on the husband and wife relationship; in light of the rosy glow of courtship, it is only natural to do so. There is usually no conscious dishonesty—the relationship is going to be perfect. The roles as stepmother or stepfather and stepchild are downplayed; everyone will just somehow adjust.

After the marriage—reality. Formerly single stepparents experience *intrusion*. They realize that they have to share their spouse with the children. The spouse is not just a wife or husband, the spouse is also a mother or father. They also find that the children, like themselves, need a great deal of space. It is particularly difficult for stepparents if their new family moves into their house, which is filled with their own belongings from their single days.

This negative experience can be avoided; many stepfamilies choose to move to a new home if they can afford it. This provides the opportunity for all family members to start off somewhat equally and will present far less difficulty regarding intrusion on the part of all family members.

Jim moved his new wife and her teenage daughter, Carolyn, into his home. There was, after all, plenty of room for them and he really hated the idea of moving. Since the house had only two bedrooms, it meant turning the one he had been using as a den back into a bedroom for Carolyn. Jim moved his large antique desk to the living room and stored all his other den furnishings and equipment in the garage until he could decide what to do with them. He did, however, leave his treaured collection of valuable books in the floor-to-ceiling bookcase. That done, he pronounced the room "All yours!" to his new stepdaughter and left the redecorating up to Carolyn and her mother.

Intrusion . . . it's a subtle feeling. In Jim's situation, he was relinquishing his comfortable den. Yet both he and Carolyn felt intruded upon. Jim felt unsettled because his belongings were not accessible to him in the garage, and he no longer had a quiet place to work.

Carolyn felt intruded on because, although she was settled into her newly decorated room, it did not feel like her own room. The books served as a constant reminder to Carolyn that the room was Jim's den.

Another aspect of intrusion concerns the previously married stepparent with children of his or her own. He or she has valued possessions and has already established guidelines concerning them that the children have learned to respect. The stepparent assumes that the new stepchildren will naturally follow these frequently unstated guidelines, but the stepparent in this situation often neglects to discuss with the stepchildren (or the new spouse) what the unspoken guidelines are. Too frequently, the intrusion occurs first—one of the stepchildren borrows something. Then, after the uproar dies down, the stepparent and parent discover they need to verbalize what the rules are.

Intrusion felt by the new stepparent can be dealt with through reeducation. Time before had been one's own, spent with whom one wished when one wished. Possessions were one's own, free from tampering by children (or spouse). In the stepfamily, stepparents must learn to share time and space with spouse and stepchildren. The motivation for learning is a strong desire to make the new relationship work.

Battling the Myths

The new stepparent usually feels pressured by the myths of stepparenthood: the wicked stepmother, the brutal stepfather, the neglectful stepmother, the miserly stepfather, the abusing stepparent. Most often, stepparents do not feel as if they start with a clean slate; they feel as if they must prove that they are not any of these awful things.

This battle may often take the form of trying to be irrefutably a "perfect" stepparent: always uncomplainingly doing all that is asked, anticipating the stepchildren's needs, satisfying their wants—no matter how unreasonable—and rearranging his or her own life to fit the stepchildren's schedule. Being a "perfect" stepparent can be exhausting. Sooner or later, the stepparent's energy wanes and the battle may be seen as lost. The loser is left feeling used and abused.

There is also the myth of instant love to contend with. Stepparents fall in love with an individual *with* children, not an individual *and* his or her children. Yet the myth of "instant love" makes stepparents feel guilty if they don't instantly love the children, too. They married to become a mate, not a stepparent. Becoming a stepparent was part of the reality of the marriage.

Wendy described this dilemma of marrying to become a wife not a stepmother...

"My husband and I had a very private and relaxed relationship for several years. Last year, his ex-wife called to inform him that his sons were coming to live with us. Mike accepted his wife's decision without consulting me! I resent my loss of privacy and the fact that Mike did not consult me when he accepted custody of the boys, but I somehow feel guilty about my resentment."

Wendy is a conscientious mother and the boys' behavior is acceptable. Since they are not a behavior problem, Wendy feels selfish about her desire for privacy and feels guilty that she wishes the boys did not exist. She feels she *should* love them. Wendy and Mike definitely have a problem to resolve.

The reality of learning to love or feel affection for stepchildren is frequently obscured by the efforts to battle the myth of instant love. The natural parent frequently has the expectation that, because the stepparent loves him or her, the stepparent will automatically love the children. Society often expects the stepparent to show love and affection for the spouse's children immediately; so, stepparents, in their efforts to please and to strengthen their marriage, muster up as many outward signs of love for their new stepchildren as they can manage. They recognize privately the fraud involved, however, and pay the price in guilt. Caught up in the myth, stepparents feel guilty that they do not immediately feel an intense love for their spouse's children. Yet love is not something that can be manufactured—it happens between two people.

No one tells stepparents that it's *okay* not to feel "instant love." Love can't often be faked; children often see the phoniness. Demonstrations of "instant love" also put the stepchildren in conflict. They are usually forced into a conflict of loyalty—stepparent versus the real parent. Often, children feel at first that they are unable to love both parent and stepparent at the same time. They don't understand that their love for others does not exist in a finite supply; they fear that by giving love to their stepparent they are taking away from their love for their real parent. The children need to mature further before they will realize the limitless quality of giving and receiving love. Rather than helping children resolve this conflict, the stepparent's false attempts to love instantly provide the children with validation. They can say, "Well, see how phony he or she is. We don't have to like him or her."

Battling these two myths can be a very vicious cycle. The harder the stepparent fights, the worse the tangle—good versus wicked, true affection versus false affection—becomes.

Stepparents must be careful to avoid the "love me, love my children" trap. Stepparents cannot and should not be expected to instantly feel love for someone else's children when they have had no time to develop such intensity of feeling.

Failure to recognize this reality creates problems. It makes everybody, including the children, feel very uncomfortable and pressured. A good love relationship has little chance of developing under such circumstances.

It is more important for stepparents to be realistic concerning the children. After all, they married their spouse for themselves, not for their children. The children were part of the package. Stepparents owe their spouse love and support; they owe their stepchildren respect.

Validation in the Role of Stepparent

Another major consideration for stepparents is their need to be validated in their role. This need will vary depending upon their position as a full-time or part-time stepparent. In many stepfamilies, stepmothers and stepfathers complain of feeling unappreciated for their efforts. An examination of the stepfamily systems in which the stepparent does feel validated for his or her efforts reveals the existence of a truly supportive and appreciative spouse.

Why this special need? The role of stepparent is often especially difficult because the individual usually does not have a model to pattern his or her behavior after. As children, most girls and boys had a mother or father who taught them what it is to be a mother or father. The children thought about growing up and being a parent, not a stepparent; they modeled their behavior on their same-sex parent's actions. Few stepmothers had a stepmother who taught them how to be a stepmother. Few stepfathers had a stepfather who taught them how to be a stepfather. They have to construct their own model for stepparenting. This process can be lengthy and may involve many mistakes along the way.

This necessity of constructing a model explains, perhaps, why so many stepparents feel a need to talk to other stepparents and compare situations. This can be useful if those involved try to work constructively on defining the boundaries of stepparenting, or it can be very destructive if those involved use the time to play "Isn't it awful..." and reinforce all the negative feelings expressed.

Assistance in achieving this model can be learned through the help of family therapy, stepparent education classes, or by joining such national organizations as Remarrieds, Inc., or The Stepfamily Foundation. The members of the latter organization are stepfamily members themselves. (More information on these organizations can be found in the concluding chapter.)

One of a stepparent's most important tasks in constructing a model is to clearly work out the boundaries of the relationship as spouse and then as stepparent. This must be an active process done jointly with one's mate.

Stepparents must recognize that their primary responsibility is to themselves, then to their role as spouse, and then to their role as stepparent. After all, they usually chose to marry to gain a mate, not to gain a ready-made family. By becoming the children's parent's spouse, they became a stepparent. Some stepparents, in their eagerness to prove the success of the marriage, take on more responsibility as a stepparent than they feel ready for. They feel unable to set limits on their role as stepparent.

Limit setting must be started prior to the remarriage and is an ongoing process of discussion. Each stepparent and spouse must explore and clarify their expectations regarding the marriage and the stepfamily. What do both partners want; what are they willing to do? Compromise will be a necessary ingredient to successful limit setting.

In a later chapter, communication techniques are discussed. These skills help facilitate this process of limit setting.

One young, single woman planned to marry a divorced man with two young sons. A month before the marriage, her fiancé's ex-wife announced that she could no longer balance the demands of her blossoming career with caring for the two boys. She brought the boys and their belongings and left them with their father. With that one action, the young woman found herself confronted not with the role of weekend stepmother, but with the role of full-time stepmother.

"I wasn't able to sit down with my fiancé and tell him how scared and unsure I felt. I didn't know if I could accept that responsibility. In fact, I really didn't want full-time custody at all. I insisted that we see a counselor. I thought that would help me and help us work something out."

With the assistance of a professional counselor, the young couple was able to construct some guidelines for the young woman's role as a full-time stepmother and some guidelines for her fiancé's full-time support and assistance. This fortified her, and she was able to face the reality of living with her fiancé and his two boys as a stepfamily.

In the foregoing example, the stepmother-to-be was able to express her doubts and admit her dismay at finding her dream of "you and me" changed to "you, me, and your kids." Other stepparents have tried to disguise their dismay or doubts because they were unable to clearly express what they're feeling. One couple who had been remarried for one year described their situation as follows:

"Before we got married, my wife seemed excited about having my children come live with us. I work irregular shifts and often must work weekends, so my time with my children has been limited. I really wanted them to live with us so I could see them more often. My wife seemed to support me in my efforts to get custody. But this past year has been sheer hell. After my children arrived, my wife seemed to change. She doesn't seem to want to get along with them and is jealous of the time I spend with them. Sometimes I feel like she's trying to get me to get rid of them."

"On the other hand, his wife said, "I guess I really didn't know what I was getting into. I'd never had any children before, so my ideas on what it would be like were pretty vague. After a few months, I realized that I was having to do all the work, all the parenting. My husband is hardly ever home; I'm left with the children

all the time. I hate having to be in charge of all the day-
to-day discipline and care. When he is around, he's all
fun and games with the children, and he ignores me."

In the above example, the stepmother does not feel
validated or appreciated in the role. Neither she nor her
husband have clarified the structure of their family and the
roles for both in parenting the children.

No One Really Wants to
Be a Stepparent? Not True!

Some stepparents find the experience both satisfying and
emotionally rewarding. They genuinely want to help their
spouse in parenting the children. One stepmother described her
satisfaction in her role:

"I had two young children by my first marriage, a
boy and a girl. I married a man with two young boys
who came to live with us two years after we were
married. I've seen some great changes in the boys since
their arrival. They were both bedwetters, were behind
in school, frequently acted out in a very destructive
way (like hitting each other over the head with a
swing), and they seemed insecure and hostile most of
the time. Over the past year, however, both boys have
settled into our home life here—it's amazing. My
children and his children get along together really
well. My son and my youngest stepson even asked to
share a room. We try to treat them as "our" children.
We deal with them as fairly as possible and tell them
constantly how much we care for them all. The boys
have stopped wetting the bed and are more relaxed and
friendly. Now we're working on helping the boys catch
up in school. Oh, we've had our ups and downs, but the
rewards of watching our family knit together and the
boys improve so much has been worth our efforts. I feel
that I can take a lot of credit for the changes since I'm
home with the children all day. I sure appreciate it,

though, when my husband comes home and takes charge of all four children. By then I need a rest!"

This stepmother had a husband who backed her up 100 percent. Some husbands make the mistake of assuming that since their wife is, after all, a woman, having children around will be no problem. They blame their wives if they are not able to handle the kids. Without a husband's support, a stepmother will feel used and resentful.

Stepparents also want appreciation from the stepchildren. When a natural parent does all the many day-to-day things that raising children involves, the natural parent often doesn't expect thanks. There is an attitude of that's what parents are for. *Or* the children have a special code to express thanks. This "secret code" is simply a system of exchange between child and parent that conveys thanks. A child may not come up to his or her parent and say, "Thank you for specially washing my favorite green T-shirt for today so I can wear it to school for my speech." But that same child may come up and lean against the parent before leaving for school. The code is usually an intangible message like this.

However, to do all of these things for someone else's children without receiving tangible thanks is another matter entirely. Stepparents want—and should receive—some thanks for their efforts. Unfortunately, they haven't had time to develop a code with their stepchildren or are unaware of the present code. So, these thank-yous may come primarily from the spouse and, at times, the stepchildren. (Some stepparents expect endless gratitude from the stepchildren who become, understandably, resentful.) The stepchildren may, in their own way, be trying to express their appreciation but with little success, since no one has initiated the stepparent into the family's code of saying thanks.

An equally important part of validation is the stepparent's desire to come first in the life of his or her mate. If stepparents feel that their spouse's first loyalty is to the children, they may feel closed out. One stepparent described this dilemma:

"When we were first married, my husband would come home from work at around six o'clock. I would go to the door and greet him and offer a kiss of welcome. As he'd lean to hug and kiss me, we'd find his little seven-year-old daughter wedged in between us clamoring to be kissed first. Sometimes he'd kiss her first and sometimes he'd kiss me first. I really resented her. It was so important to me to be kissed first ... after all, I was his wife. This silent struggle went on for six months before I finally told my husband how I felt. He understood, and from that day on, I got kissed first. He sat down and explained to his daughter that she was very special and that he looked forward to seeing her each evening when he got home. But he wanted her to wait her turn, and she was able to accept the situation."

Perhaps the most important ingredient to success and validation as a stepparent is a strong self-image. An individual with a shaky sense of self and a weak estimation of worth is going to have trouble making it as a stepparent.

Stepparents must be secure in the knowledge of their own worth and value. Their self-image must be able to withstand all the many situations that seem to conspire to make them doubt their capabilities. Stepparents will make mistakes and meet drawbacks in their attempts to construct a model for themselves. They will encounter situations in which their needs and wants will seem to come last, where they are made to feel unimportant, or where they are made to feel that their efforts are valueless.

To withstand these pressures, stepparents' self-esteem must be very high. They must be able to assert their worth to themselves, their spouse, their children and stepchildren, and the community.

Learning to Discipline

Part of learning how to make the new steprelationship work is learning how to discipline stepchildren. Formerly single stepparents have at their disposal the wealth of knowledge gained over the years by their spouse. They undoubtedly have ideas of their own on parenting, but these ideas need to be blended with the discipline strategies of the stepchildren's parent.

Children inevitably test to see just what the new limits are—both in the case of the "superparent" and in the case of the "reluctant stepparent." Frequently, stepparents react by trying to prove that they are in control, that they can get the children to do what they want. The harder they try to prove themselves, the more diligently the children test.

Where does this cycle of behavior lead? It usually leads to a no-win situation if the following occurs: The child misbehaves, the stepparent tries to discipline the child, the child is unhappy with the discipline and complains to the natural parent, the natural parent sides with the child, the stepparent feels that his or her actions have been undermined. Unwittingly, the natural parent has discouraged the stepparent from playing a vital role as a parent. The natural parent has created a triangle, blocking interaction between stepparent and stepchild.

Stepparents typically resent being the odd person out in the triangle. They share in providing a home and financial support, but have no say in setting up the structure of authority and discipline in the home. They are frustrated in a position outside the family circle. In this unhappy triangle, the natural parent is perpetuating a single-parent family structure. Messages are sent from parent to child and from child to parent. The stepparent has no direct communication channel to the stepchildren.

A possible consequence of this cycle is that most stepparent/stepchild interaction shrinks. The irony is this: The natural parent has set the situation up, yet may become unhappy at the stepparent's lack of involvement with the children and blame the stepparent for withdrawing.

This frustrating cycle cannot occur if parent and stepparent sit down in the beginning stages of their relationship and discuss their perceptions of discipline. They should address the following issues: What types of discipline has the natural

parent used in the past? What types of discipline did the
absentee parent use if different from the natural parent? What
are the stepparent's expectations concerning discipline in the
home? How much of a role is the stepparent willing to play in
disciplining the stepchildren? How much of a role is the natural
parent willing to allow the stepparent to play? Are they willing
to back one another up 100 percent?

"How to discipline" is very different from "what to
discipline." The "what" of disciplining will be discussed later
in a chapter on discipline. It is important to note here that
parent and stepparent must be in relative agreement on what is
and is not desirable behavior.

The goal of this discussion is to achieve a system of
discipline and cooperative effort to achieve a comfortable
family structure. The children can function securely within the
limits set up by the parent and stepparent. There is no need to
continue testing; they know exactly because these expectations
have been clearly outlined for them by a united parent and
stepparent. The stepparent will not feel compelled to prove that
he or she is in charge and the natural parent will not
inadvertently encourage distance between spouse and children
by taking sides.

The preceding discussion mainly concerned the formerly
single stepparent. Obviously, stepparents with children of their
own by a previous marriage have had experience disciplining
their own children. Many times they feel the same methods will
work with their stepchildren. Again, prior discussion and
blending of ideas is necessary. Stepparents must address with
the natural parent all of the questions outlined previously.
They would add the concern: How do they discipline their own
children? How do they want their spouse to discipline their
children? These precautions will ensure a balance of discipline.

Stepparent's Dilemma

One of the more difficult aspects of the stepparent's role is
the dilemma concerning his or her own children. Stepparents
are caught in a bind when they are full-time stepparents yet

only part-time natural parents. They find themselves in the position of taking care of someone else's children most of the time, yet they are only able to care for their own children some of the time.

A natural consequence of this dilemma is often guilt. Feelings of guilt center around the stepparent's inability to spend time with and support his or her own children in the same manner that he or she does with his or her stepchildren.

These guilt feelings may lead to overcompensation on the part of the stepparent. Jim, a forty-year-old stepfather, had difficulty resolving his dilemma.

> Jim has two teen-age sons, fifteen and seventeen, from his first marriage. He's been divorced from their mother for eight years. Three years ago, he married a woman with a girl and a boy, now twelve and fourteen years old. Jim is the sole support of his stepfamily and also pays child support and alimony to his ex-wife. Jim had never successfully resolved being an absentee father.
>
> "I always feel guilty about not being able to spend more time with my two sons. I'm lucky that I'm able to have them over every weekend; but during their weekend visits, I just can't bring myself to discipline them. My time with them is so limited that I just don't want to spoil the weekend by having to come down on them too hard. So, I let a lot of things like bad language or disrespect for my wife slide by. Yet, if my two teen-agers who live with me get out of line, I really let them have it."

This lack of discipline resulted in an uneven, seemingly unfair family structure. The two natural children were deprived of the structure and guidance that their natural father could provide if he chose to discipline them when they were out of line. The stepchildren saw this imbalance and did not see its source; they only saw the resulting favoritism. Frequently, Jim took the two boys sailing on the weekends. His wife and stepchildren

felt excluded and resentful of this special privilege accorded the
visiting sons. They felt he was giving more energy, time, and
money to his natural children than to his stepfamily.

    What was not clearly understood by Jim or by his wife and
stepchildren was Jim's underlying motive for this behavior. He
was with his stepfamily daily and was without his sons except
on a weekend basis. His solution had been to try to create a
balance by setting aside time alone with his sons.

    What seemed like favoritism was actually an attempt to
compensate. Jim's wife and stepchildren saw the imbalance
from their perspective and Jim saw it from his. What Jim did
not realize was that it was only *natural* to feel pinched by this
bind. By handling the situation the way he did, however, he
was not dealing with his guilt and was destroying his
stepfamily.

    The solution in this stepfamily was to find a balance to
relieve feelings of guilt and resentment. Jim was able to deal
with this dilemma by spending one or two weekends doing
things like sailing alone with his two sons and including his
two stepchildren and wife on any outings the other two
weekends. This enabled him to give his full attention to his sons
on their solo weekends and promote stepfamily unity on the
other two weekends. He also arranged to spend time with his
two sons one evening a week; he was able to meet them right
after work, have dinner together, and enjoy some activity or,
often, just spend a quiet evening with them at home. With this
increased contact with his sons, Jim was able to feel less guilty
and compensate less by letting inappropriate behavior slide by.
He chose to discipline, and his sons responded positively to the
change.

Dealing with the Stepchildren's Absentee Parent

    While the ex-spouse may be part of the past in the new
husband-wife relationship, the absentee parent is still very
much a part of the present in the children's lives. The absentee
parent may be deceased or living far away, but he or she may
remain as important an influence in the children's lives as does

the parent with whom they are living. Stepparents make a prime mistake when they fail to reckon with this.

Stepparents must avoid putting down their stepchildren's absentee parent. This may be extremely hard in situations in which the absentee parent is irresponsible, inconsistent in visitation, or uses child support payments—sends the money late or not at all—as a vehicle for harassment. In these instances, it would be very tempting for the stepparent to make derogatory remarks about the absentee parent.

It is really unnecessary to say anything. Actions speak much louder than words. The children will realize as they mature who is consistent and concerned with their welfare. Until that maturity is reached, the children will undoubtedly say things like, "You're not my real parent!" or "My real parent wouldn't do that!" At times like these, stepparents may have to bite back that derogatory remark or refrain from pointing out all that they do for the stepchildren. Again, forbearance pays off in the long run.

This promise of a later payoff may seem like a poor reward to the stepparent. However, here is a situation where the adult must act as a responsible parent. There is no real gain (only a temporary gratification) to be realized by confronting the child with the reality of an irresponsible, possibly indifferent, absentee parent. The child, not the absentee parent, is harmed by the derogatory remarks. The child's self-esteem, not the absentee parent's, is irreparably damaged.

In the situation in which the natural parent is deceased, the stepparent's task is slightly different. The child usually has an idealized image of the natural parent who has died. The stepparent will find it very hard to compete against this idealized "saint." The mere human is at a definite disadvantage as he or she makes human mistakes.

A stepparent will find it helpful in this case to acknowledge the child's natural parent and confirm this importance in the child's memory. Stepparents should make it clear to the child that they are *not* trying to take the place of the natural parent, indeed it would be difficult to do so. There can be only two biological parents. This honesty will promote open communication and make it easier for the child to retain a

satisfactory memory of the parent while still developing a close
relationship with the stepparent.

One thirty-five-year-old stepfather dealt with this situation in the following way:

> Larry had been married to his wife for ten years and
> had a thirteen-year-old stepson and an eight-year-old
> natural daughter. His stepson's dad, a pilot, had been
> killed when the boy was two years old. At thirteen, the
> boy was showing a great deal of interest in his natural
> father. At first, Larry felt hurt by this interest because
> he, after all, had been the boy's "father" for the past ten
> years. After giving it some thought, Larry decided that
> his stepson had a right to know more about his real
> father. He found a picture of the boy's father,
> resplendent in his pilot's uniform, framed it, and gave
> it to the boy to put in his room. He also encouraged his
> wife to tell her son about his real father—what he was
> like, how the boy was similar to his father, and what
> experiences father and son had shared before the
> father's death. Secure in his new-found knowledge, the
> boy was able to appreciate his stepfather's efforts.

Having Another Child

Many stepparents who never had a child of their own face
the difficult problem of wanting to have a child. Yet the
question is changed from, "Are we ready for a child?" or, "Can
we afford to start a family?" to the question, "Are we ready for
another child!" or, "Can we afford to have a larger family?"
This issue can be an emotional battlefield for both the natural
parent and the stepparent in the stepfamily.

There is no easy solution. If the stepparent is the
stepmother, her childbearing years are limited, and the
decision can only be debated for a finite number of years.
Regardless of whether the stepparent is a stepmother or
stepfather, the issue of resentment—of feeling cheated out of
the "real thing," biological parenthood—must be dealt with.

Both husband and wife need to question their reasons for
wanting a child. Agreeing to have a child to appease one's

spouse or wanting one in order to "come first" with at least one member of the family are not good reasons for having a child. Other considerations are the ages and needs of the rest of the family members.

> Lori married Terry, the widowed father of four sons aged six, eight, nine, and eleven. They had been married for two years.
>
> "I had always planned on having children. My dream as I was growing up was to live in the country and have several children. I guess it never occurred to me that I would fall in love with a man who already had four children! We've talked and talked about having a child, one that will be ours completely, but Terry feels strongly that four boys are quite enough. I agree that four children are plenty, but I want to bear our child, be part of creating and raising another human being. We haven't resolved this issue yet, but I'm hopeful that we'll be able to reach a solution. Terry would be thrilled to have a daughter..."

Guidelines for Stepparents

1. *Be yourself.* Don't be defensive about the myths of the cruel stepparent. Your own natural actions are your best offense.

2. *Be a spouse first and a stepparent second.* Your first responsibility is to yourself, then to your marriage, then to your responsibilities as a stepparent. Refuse to allow yourself to be pressured into reversing these priorities.

3. *Be honest.* It's okay to admit that you don't love your stepchildren. Your marriage depends on the bond between you and your mate. The children's sanction of the marriage is not necessary. You owe your stepchildren respect for their place in the family. Love and affection must be allowed time to develop.

4. *Assert yourself; you need to be valued.* Ask for 100 percent acknowledgment of your role as stepparent. Be open with your spouse about your need for full support and appreciation. Don't wait for him or her to "see the light." Sit down with your fiancée or, if already married, your mate; and

explore the boundaries of your relationship as a stepparent.

5. *Define your limits.* "This is how much of an active parenting role I am willing to play..."

6. *Risk asserting authority.* Be confident and work with your spouse to exchange ideas on how to best parent the children. Make this a joint effort.

7. *Be open to compromise.* Children need space and the freedom to act like children. They should not be made to feel like intruders among your possessions and in your home. Use foresight and planning to avoid feelings of intrusion.

8. *Be honest with yourself before marrying a person with children.* If you're willing to be a stepparent, be realistic that parenting someone else's children will not be easy. It is not the same as running a business. If you're not willing to be a stepparent, do not marry a person with children. Marrying anyway and then refusing to recognize your role as stepparent will make it very difficult to find happiness in the marriage.

9. *Ask for understanding and opportunities to ventilate.* Let your spouse know that there are times you just need him or her to *listen* without becoming defensive. You need to complain and discuss the difficulties of being a stepparent; clarify that you are letting off steam, not attacking. Once you've let off steam, you can discuss how to solve the issues.

10. *Learn the "secret code."* Ask your spouse and stepchildren to teach you the secret code, that exchange of behaviors they've developed to express appreciation. Don't let aggravation or resentment build because you've been missing their attempts to let you know you're appreciated.

11. *Be realistic about the past.* Accept the reality of your spouse's past and remind yourself that if his or her ex-spouse or previous family truly came first, he or she would still be married to the ex-spouse or still be living alone as a single parent. Your new spouse married you because he or she wanted to. Do not make the past family system an unmentionable subject.

12. *Question your reasons for having a child.* Remind yourself that you will be bringing a child into this world who deserves to have *two* loving parents and a warm and secure home.

VI
The Child
in the Stepfamily

Each year, more and more parents are remarrying. Much of the success of these relationships depends on the clear role definition of parent and stepparent. A clear definition of the role of the child in the stepfamily greatly enhances the longevity of the remarriage. (See diagram on page 78.)

The children are placed in the middle, surrounded by the four major areas of role definition. This is the way children view the world: egocentrically, revolving around self. The children experience the world as happening in relation to themselves. The family is their world; its breakdown creates a dark void, shattering their sense of self and undermining feelings of security.

The Child's Heritage

The first aspect of role definition for children in the stepfamily is their *heritage*. Children bring to the blended family a heritage of pain and confusion. They have experienced the pain of losing a parent and fear losing their remaining parent. They may wonder, "Will this new adult take my parent away from me?" They may still be confused about their parents' divorce and refuse to accept its permanence. This loss and insecurity can be minimized by support and nurturance from the remaining parent and stepparent.

Stepchildren carry into their new family systems a heritage of aloneness and, perhaps, helplessness that they picked up from the single parent during the interim period. The parent and stepparent should reassure their children that they will be there to care for them and that they intend to make this new relationship permanent.

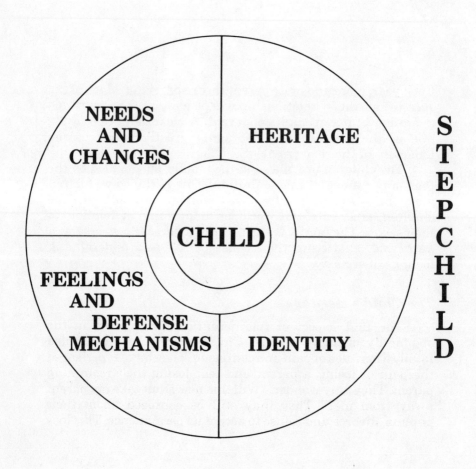

Children often bring to their new families roles played in the old family system. If there was conflict in the previous family, the children may have learned certain behaviors to deal with the unhappiness. These behaviors are not appropriate in their new stepfamilies and must be unlearned.

Bill, a twelve-year-old, had learned to distract his parents whenever they fought bitterly. He found that he could sidetrack his parents by stealing. He always got caught immediately. His mother and father would focus all of their attention on him, momentarily forgetting their differences. Naturally, at the first sign of disharmony between his parent and stepparent, he attempted to cope by distracting ... with unfortunate results.

Bill's behavior was seen as problematic and inappropriate. He was disciplined firmly and left feeling confused—it had worked before, hadn't it? He needed help learning new behavior and needed reassurance that one fight would not mean the end of his parent's remarriage. Fortunately, Bill's natural parent realized after a time the connection between Bill's behavior now and previous learning. Once he explained what he expected from Bill in the present stepfamily, he and Bill were able to work things out.

The Child's Identity

The second area that children and parents must explore in the role definition is the aspect of *identity*. The children's identity lies with both natural parents. From their biological parents, children derive a sense of who they are, what they are like, and what their relation is to the world. Having experienced parental conflict, divorce, the interim period, and the single-parent family, the children may bring to their stepfamilies a shaky sense of self and insecurity. Within a steady, stable structure of a stepfamily, the children can recover.

There are several pitfalls parents can avoid to assist their stepchildren's recovery. Parents can avoid any putdowns or discounts of the children's absentee parent. A putdown of the biological parent is a putdown of the child.

This issue often raises painful questions for the natural parent with custody. How much do I tell my child about his or her real parent? Many natural parents agonize this question; perhaps the absentee parent is irresponsible and self-centered, hasn't visited the children in months, and is ducking child support responsibilities. Sometimes the step or natural parent's first inclination is to really let the child have the full details. This often results in comments like, "He or she doesn't care about you," or "Your parent is no good." These statements, though they may possibly be true, are very harmful to the child's developing self-esteem and *should be avoided*.

A general rule of thumb is this: Only tell as much of the truth as the children are old enough to understand and need to know. There is no need to lie, but neither is there any need to burden the children's developing self-esteem. As they grow older, they will discover the truth for themselves. Many stepparents or natural parents rationalize this issue by saying, "Well, I was only being realistic for the children's own good." Rather, so the parent or stepparent will feel better!

A second pitfall to be avoided concerns the children's sense of importance, which is a part of identity. Part of a single parent's job was to set up the structure of parent/child. As the adult, a parent should make the decision to remarry; as a child, the son or daughter should be told of the parent's decision before the remarriage takes place. The children *should not have* the power to approve or reject the parent's decision to remarry.

This is not to say that the children's feelings or opinions are ignored. After all, their parent's decision to remarry drastically affects their lives. Parents must allow the children to express their opinions, they should reflect the children's feelings: "You're really worried and anxious about what it's going to be like..." Understanding and warmth are crucial.

Many single parents feel that they actually need their children's approval and okay to remarry. How many children are capable of handling that much power? Again, it is the parent's decision to remarry—not the children's decision.

Feelings and Defense Mechanisms

An important area to consider when defining step-children's roles can be grouped under feelings and defense mechanisms.

Perhaps one of the most difficult problems stepchildren must deal with is the *loyalty conflict*. Many stepchildren feel caught between their feelings of love and identification with the natural parent who is absent and their growing respect (possibly even love) for and identification with the stepparent. For most, it is often described as an either/or proposition. They are caught in the middle.

Younger children may somehow feel disloyal to their natural parent if they admit that they care about the stepparent. After all, they've got to stick by their natural parent. Absentee parents may foster this loyalty conflict by subtly encouraging the children to express negative feelings about the stepparent. Absentee parents may also express hurt or rejection if the children express positive feelings about the stepparent.

It is as though love came in a bucket that could only hold a limited amount. If the young child draws some out to give the stepparent, there will be less in the bucket for the natural parent; or worse, the bucket may be empty! Young children need to be taught that love is in endless supply—that the more love a child gives and receives, the more love there is still to give. The bucket never empties.

It is important to note that children do not have to love their stepparent. Respect, yes. Love, no. Many stepchildren feel forced by their custody parent to express love for their stepparent, either verbally or physically. By expecting children to immediately love their stepparent, their parent makes the children feel uncomfortable and risks alienating them. Love can't be forced.

Stepchildren may often feel *bewildered*. During the years spent as a nuclear family and then as a single-parent family, the children learned behaviors or ways of reacting to parents. When their mother or father did "that," they did "this." These

learned behaviors may not be appropriate when being parented
by a new stepparent. Young children may be bewildered when
reprimanded, saying, "Gee, we always did it that way."
Stepparent and children need time to learn how to be parent
and child together.

All people have defense mechanisms, ways of coping with
changes, stress, and anxiety. Children are no exception; they
learn coping behaviors that help them deal with life. These
coping mechanisms can be healthy and helpful, or they can be
unhealthy with undesirable results like the *acting out* in the
following example.

> One young boy of six, Jason, was referred for
> counseling by his worried father and stepmother. He
> and his brother came to live with their father and
> stepmother four months ago. His father, stepmother,
> and stepmother's two children, aged four and five, had
> been living as a family for one year. Both parent and
> stepparent were quite worried because their son was
> acting out: throwing temper tantrums, and hitting his
> brother over the head with toys. During the counseling,
> it became apparent that this boy of six had lived in
> *twelve* different family systems before coming to live
> with his father. He had lived with his natural mother
> and father, grandmother, grandfather and grand-
> mother, mother alone, mother and girlfriend, mother
> and boyfriend, and so on. His method of coping with all
> the changes was by acting out. As soon as his father
> and stepmother were able to prove to him (no easy
> task) that their home was the final stop, not just the
> thirteenth situation, the young boy stopped acting out.
> He had needed two things: (1) proof that his father
> would not let him down, and (2) time to settle in, to feel
> that home was permanent.

Another defense mechanism is *displacement*. Many
children feel angry at their absentee parent for leaving them or
for not visiting more often. Yet, since time with their absentee
parent may be limited and at a premium, the children may find

it difficult to express anger directly. They may instead dump it on the next "logical" choice—their stepparent. The stepparent, if tuned in to this coping device, can handle this misdirected anger in an adult manner—recognizing it for what it is and not striking back. This places the responsibility on the adult in the situation. Parents can help children learn to recognize misdirected anger by reflecting the anger and allowing for its source.

Withdrawal is a third type of defense mechanism used by children. Withdrawal is a quiet, nonverbal battle in which the children not only pit themselves against their stepparent but also against their entire family. The children often withdraw from interaction with their family by isolating themselves in their room or by becoming extremely involved in outside interests.

> John, a fifteen-year-old, was very actively involved in family activities prior to his mother's remarriage. He was unhappy about the divorce and opposed to the remarriage. He coped with the situation by withdrawing from his family. He filled his waking hours with more than the usual amount of teen-age activities at school and elsewhere. He came home only to sleep and made no effort to communicate with parent or stepparent. He refused to participate in any activity with parents by always having at hand some important event. No overt refusal, just a subtle "I'm really busy." His method of coping was to withdraw from any family involvement.

John's solution only exacerbated the problem, however. Since he was rarely around, neither he nor his parent and stepparent had any opportunities to resolve their differences.

A fourth much-used defense mechanism is *psychosomatic illness*. In this situation, the children's symptoms may be very real. They have headaches, stomachaches, flu-like aches and pains, vomiting, or diarrhea. These are real ... but they are not due to a virus or other medical reason. The children are attempting to deal with stress or anxiety by escaping into sickness. The payoff in this situation is that they get to stay home and receive a lot of attention from their parents. This illness defense mechanism was illustrated rather dramatically by one twelve-year-old girl, Julie.

Julie lived with her natural mother, stepfather, and brother. Her natural father, stepmother, and their six-month-old baby lived in a nearby city. Julie, a new seventh-grader, was having a difficult time adjusting to the demands of a large junior high school. Her reaction was to have frequent stomachaches on the evenings before school and on school mornings. Julie's mother took her to a doctor for a complete physical. His response, "She's in perfect health." Julie also had another problem: She wanted to go and live with her father. Her way of coping was an attempt to manipulate her parents to get her way. What Julie did was to cry—deep, heartrending, gut-wrenching sobs. She did this every morning and during school, breaking into tears unpredictably and at any time.

The result of Julie's behavior was that she spent a good part of the day in the counselor's office. The counselor tried to cope with the problem by trying to be understanding, trying to talk to the girl despite her sobbing—all with no results. In desperation, she met with Julie's mother, then with her mother and stepfather, then with the natural father, and, finally, with her natural father and stepmother. The counselor found all four adults were giving the girl four different messages about the family situation, where she should live, and about the problem of crying. They each had their own private perception of the problem and possible solution.

Julie's natural father feared that the crying was a sign of deep psychological disturbance. However, the counselor had noticed that Julie could turn the crying on and off at will. In fact, she never cried during one particular class. (That teacher had said from the start that she would not stand for it and that Julie was to knock it off.)

The counselor got all four parents together and instructed

them on the importance of presenting just one message: "Your home is with your mother and that's where you will stay. There will be no change at this time nor any change in the near future. Stop the crying!"

The crying stopped at home when Julie realized it would not persuade her parents. She did, however, continue to cry at school as a way of coping with the strangeness of the new school setting. The counselor began by instructing Julie that she was not allowed to cry during class. All her teachers gave Julie the same message; so, Julie went to the counselor during her lunch hour to cry instead. Gradually, the counselor taught Julie to express her feelings by talking and taught her more effective ways of dealing with her family situation. She accepted the fact that her parents had the power to choose the best home situation for her.

Many stepparents complain of hearing the refrain, "If you were my real parent..." This can be a stepchild's last-ditch effort to cope. Backed into a corner, the stepchild can defiantly, and very factually, point out this truth. It is quite true that if the stepchild's real parent were at hand, things would be different. In children's minds, this gets them off the hook, releases them from their responsibility to deal with the situation. They can fantasize that the world would be better "if..."

This fantasy goes hand in hand with the fantasy of mother and father getting back together. Despite all evidence, many children hang on to this belief until some final sign that it's over. Others never relinquish the fantasy without the help of parents and counselors. One mother described her surprise when confronted with this fantasy.

"One night my two boys, eleven and thirteen, were sitting around watching television. I'd been remarried for three years, and my husband, Ben, and the boys got along pretty well. They visited their real father once a month for the weekend and two months every summer. Anyway, they were watching television in one room while I was working in a nearby room. I overheard my eleven-year-old describing to my thirteen-year-old how great it was going to be when "we" all lived together

again in their old house. He didn't seem to realize that
the divorce was permanent.

"The next day I found a good chance to talk with him
by asking him to help me out in the garden. While we
worked, I told him that I had overheard him last night
and understood how he felt, that he would really like it
if things could be the way he wanted. But I let him
know as gently as I could that it wasn't going to
happen. His father and I both loved the boys dearly,
but we couldn't ever live together again as a family. I
tried to describe how happy I was with Ben and how we
all got along together well as a stepfamily. I think he
understood... and we hugged each other to end the
conversation."

Needs and Changes

A parent's remarriage brings to the forefront special
needs. Children need assurance and reassurance that their
custodial parent will "be there" to meet their needs, provide
love and warmth, make a home for the family. The children
have already "lost" one family maker through death or divorce.
The parent's remarriage may bring back fears and memories of
the previous loss. Children need reassurance that they are
wanted and will be an important part of the new family system.

Children also need at least one consistent, reliable, and
dependable parenting figure. This is usually the natural parent
with custody. Sometimes, though, it may be a stepparent.

One stepmother described her situation in which she was
the only reliable, consistent parenting figure in her two
stepchildren's lives:

"During the winter months the children lived with
their mother but were actually cared for by a
combination of baby-sitters and relatives. Their mother interacted very little with them. During the
summer, they stayed with their father and me; but
Frank was frequently busy and showed little interest
in them. I have a genuine affection for the two of them

and try to provide a stable, warm home for them during the summer months—actively parenting for that time. I frequently call or write during the winter months."

Children in a stepfamily face many changes due to a parent's remarriage such as new family members, new surroundings, and new ways of doing things. They may be fearful at first because these changes are unknown. They need information about how the changes will affect them.

One young boy expressed a constant anxiety over his father's impending remarriage. He kept asking worriedly about what chores would be expected of him in the new family situation. He pestered his father and stepmother-to-be about the specific chores, when they would have to be done, whether or not he would be punished if he did an unsatisfactory job. His father became worried after several weeks of this seemingly excessive focus on chores and sought the assistance of a counselor.

Together, the counselor and boy arrived at the underlying source of the anxiety. What the boy really wanted to ask but didn't know how was, "If the new situation is as bad as the old one, will I be stuck?" He wanted to know what help would be available to him if his father and stepmother fought as much as his father and mother had. Armed with the counselor's telephone number in case of a future emergency, the boy felt confident to face the unknown changes. He never needed to use that telephone number.

Other changes involve the family name, family traditions, number of siblings, number of relatives, birth order, houses, schools, bedrooms, eating habits, and so on with an endless list. Many times these changes seem minor to an adult but loom large to the children. Children must often deal with their parent having a different name and endure the embarrassment of the constant mix-ups that can occur. An oldest child must adjust to suddenly being a middle child, or a youngest child, or must deal with a younger stepsibling taking his or her position. Things like moving over to make room in a bedroom or a closet all mean some adjustment. They all require *time* and *space*.

Children in a stepfamily need time to adjust to all the changes and also space to deal with them. We all need some space that we can call our own, territory that is "ours" and respected by all. Children are no different.

The visiting stepchild especially needs this special space. How difficult it is to visit one's own parent at his or her house and have to sleep on the floor in a sleeping bag in the stepsibling's bedroom. Visiting children need to feel especially welcome by having their own place in the toothbrush holder, their own bedroom, if possible, their own bed, their own drawer for their clothes. They should not have to feel like a visitor: They are a member of the family with a place in that family system.

Most children in step who shift between homes need to know that one home is their "home base." They need the freedom to grow within the consistent, stable structure of that home. The child whose parents frequently shift custody depending on the ups and downs of child-rearing often feels like he or she has no real home and never learns to be successful in a setting. Children in this situation learn instead that when things get rough, they can always pack up and go live with the other parent. This lesson often follows children through life. They never really deal with major problems—they just move on. Children need to belong.

As the children shift between their home base and their home with the absentee parent, they will experience a phenomenon called *reorientation*. Just before the child leaves, he or she usually psyches up for the new situation. Upon return, he or she gears back down. The child has to reorient to each home and situation. Many stepparents or parents describe those hours before and after a visit as unpredictable, yet understandable. Both homes have different people and different ways of doing things, and the children must be "expert" in discriminating between the two. This requires some skill. It is easiest when both parent and absentee parent have managed cooperatively to set up similar family structures.

It is also easier when the children are allowed to be neutral in both family camps. The adjustment to coming and going is easier if they know that they will not be questioned about the other parent's friends and activities. It is easier if they are not pressured to take sides or give information. Again, consistency and fairness can eliminate the disruptions natural to visiting back and forth.

Guidelines for Parents of Children in a Stepfamily

1. *Be perceptive.* Consider the children's legacy from the past and examine what their roles were in their previous families and single-parent families.

2. *Use discretion.* Don't put down the children's parent or share negative feelings or comments with them unnecessarily. It is okay for the children to believe in the absentee parent, despite that parent's failings. Do not give the children power to sign for or veto the remarriage. Your discretion can help foster healthy development of their identity.

3. *Learn to reflect your child's feelings.* Tune in to the feelings rather than just the contents of your children's messages. Talk with them about love, emphasizing its limitless quality. Let your children know that you expect them to show respect for the stepparent. At the same time, let them know that they do not have to instantly love the stepparent.

4. *Plan the stepfamily.* Plan how things are to be done in the new family system. Don't wait until everyone is confused about how things used to be done versus how things are to be done now.

5. *Deal effectively with coping mechanisms.* Learn to recognize coping mechanisms, and teach your children more appropriate ways of dealing with stress, such as talking, expressing negative and positive feelings, and asking for help. Remove the payoff for the inappropriate behavior and reward a more appropriate behavior. One mother whose daughter frequently became "ill" refused to let her stay home from school. She did, however, make it a practice to pick her

daughter up from school once a week, without the younger
children along. On the way home, they would stop for a soda
and some time alone together. There the mother would
encourage her daughter to express her feelings about the family
situation, school, and friends and would help her daughter
work through any problems that had arisen during the week.
Her daughter really enjoyed having her mother's undivided
attention; her mother enjoyed the time she could give her
daughter free from demands from other family members.

6. *Response to "If you were my real parent..."* Respond to
this statement with warm understanding of the child's point of
view. "You are right, I'm not your real parent, and I can't take
the place of your parent. Here in this house we do it this way,
however."

7. *Provide reassurance.* Don't be too busy to provide the
reassurance children need that you will be there for them when
they need you. Be the consistent, stable parent in the children's
lives.

8. *Help minimize changes.* Help the children by minimiz-
ing the number of changes brought about by the remarriage. Do
all that you can to ensure that the children feel that they have a
valuable place in the family system.

9. *Be understanding.* Be understanding of the difficulties
children encounter in going back and forth between visits.
Learn to recognize problems brought on by the expected
reorientation period.

10. *Support neutrality.* Give your children the gift of
allowing them to be neutral. Do not involve them in your
feelings of bitterness or animosity toward your ex-spouse. The
children did not choose to divorce the parent.

11. *Form a united front.* Unite as a parenting team. If both
natural parent and stepparent are together regarding discipline, respect, and setting limits, being a stepchild is less
complicated. Children know what is expected of them because
the messages come directly from both parents. They then
realize (possibly after testing the parental bond) that there are
limits, that they are cared for, and that they have a place in the
family. Once this is accomplished, the family can operate in a
more comfortable manner.

Adolescence

"You're always on my case. You don't like my hair, you don't like my clothes, you don't like my friends—I wish I could move out and get an apartment with somebody. Then nobody could hassle me. I could get a job and quit school. School is a drag. Who cares what a bunch of dead guys did two hundred years ago? You don't need to know that kind of stuff to get a job.

"By the way, do you think I could have the car tonight? A bunch of us want to go to the drive-in. What do you mean? I cleaned the garage today. Just go look—it's clean! You mean I was supposed to *sweep* it too? You never said I had to sweep too. You guys treat me like some kind of slave or something.

"You never do anything for me."

If these words sound familiar, you are most probably a parent with an adolescent child. If your child is grown and you have somehow made it through this trying period, you are more than likely still carrying some battle scars. On the other hand, if you have not yet been on the receiving end of a conversation like the one above, but you have noticed a sharp tone creeping into your preadolescent child's voice during his or her conversations with you and discovered that the old tried and true disciplinary methods suddenly don't work as well as they used to—then this discussion will be of interest to you.

This discussion will not attempt to cover in great detail all of the problems of adolescence; the subject is far too complex to deal with effectively in a book of this nature. Instead, we will attempt to identify some of the major stumbling blocks that parents, and particularly stepparents, encounter during the adolescent period. We will offer guidance on dealing with adolescents, but both natural and stepparents might wish to seek further information from a book specializing in adolescent development.

It is necessary to deal with the particular problems associated with adolescence for two reasons. One, these problems that are faced by both parent and adolescent are common in most Western cultures. Two, previous books dealing

with stepfamily relationships do not differentiate between the
child in the stepfamily and the adolescent in the stepfamily.

A family relationship that involves a stepparent and an
adolescent presents a particularly difficult problem much
different from any problems encountered by a stepparent and a
younger child. But first, a clear understanding of adolescence—
its history and specific developmental difficulties for teen-ager
and parent—is necessary. Only through this understanding
can parents and adolescents arrive at some possible solutions
or coping behaviors. Once parents, single parents, and
stepparents achieve such an understanding, they will be more
successful in helping both themselves and their children
through this turbulent period of change.

Adolescence is officially that period from age twelve to age
twenty-one, although it may last longer. It may seem to both
parent and child to be a combination of the Hundred Years'
War because it feels like it will never end and may feel like a
United Nations meeting because no one seems to be able to
agree. It is a period of confusion for both adolescent and parent.
The young person often feels entitled to adult privileges,
independence, and freedom. The parent, on the other hand,
sometimes sees these needs—often expressed in the form of
demands—as unrealistic and unreasonable.

Many adolescent difficulties are created by changes in
society. Our Western society or culture has placed the
adolescent in an artificially prolonged "holding pattern"
between ceasing to be a dependent child and becoming a
responsible adult. Adolescence continues through the late teens
and early twenties despite the fact that the teen-ager/young
adult has been physically and, sometimes, emotionally mature
for some time. Yet, the prolonged educational requirements of
our culture and the economic difficulties in setting up an
independent household maintain the adolescent in a prolonged
dependency on parents—a holding pattern.

History of Adolescence

By way of contrast, today's counterpart adolescent in the
1800s was usually a somewhat efficient, independent, and

capable individual. Young males fought wars, supported families, farmed the land, explored new territories, and made important decisions affecting not only the family but also the community. The female, although hampered by the restrictions on the activities of women that were prevalent at that time, still endured the hardships of settling the West, establishing homes, and rearing and educating their children.

Even with the onset of industrialization and the subsequent move away from the farm and into the cities, there was still a place in the job market for young people in this age group. There was a nearly insatiable need for labor by the newly emerging industries.

Up until about thirty years ago there were few jobs that adolescents could not handle as well as adults. This was due, in part, to the proliferation of jobs that required little education and technical skill. With the advent of the space age, jobs required an increasingly higher degree of education and skill. This development, coupled with a dramatic increase in the number of applicants in the job pool who possessed this education and technical skill, effectively eliminated most adolescents from the job market. Thus, economic independence became increasingly impossible to achieve and adolescents were forced to remain dependent upon parents for a longer period of time.

The adolescents of today are no less innately capable of achieving independence, acting responsibly, successfully holding down a job, and competing with adults in other areas of life than were their counterparts of a hundred years ago. Adolescents today, however, find that society often has no place for them in the adult world; as a result, they lack the sense of individual identity that is so essential to the maturing process. All the tasks that help individuals define their place in society—the successful performance of a job that provides economic independence, carrying out of marriage and family responsibilities—are denied today's adolescents, and nothing has been provided to take the place of these things. It is as if the adult world has closed its doors on that group of individuals whose ages span from approximately twelve to twenty-one.

Today's Adolescent

In contrast to young people as recently as one generation ago, today's adolescents spend a major portion of their time in school—often sitting day after day through hours of classes that may seem to have no relevance to their daily lives. Adolescents today have the same desire and need for independence and identity as people in that age group have always had. Now, however, one of the most important means of obtaining that independence and identity—the job—is, frequently, no longer available. It is no wonder that adolescents experience frustration and anger in their search for a place in society. To add to this frustration, today's adolescents are part of a generation that has grown up with television. Impressionable adolescents have been exposed to an enormous amount of media hype, such as a group of teen-agers cruising around at the beach in a new toy—a brand-new automobile. The media blitz creates a craving for a wide variety of luxuries at a time in life in which the ability to obtain these things is severely restricted by enforced dependence upon parents (unless the parents are willing to satisfy the teen-agers, every new "I want..."). The end result of this exposure in the face of economic dependence may be anger, frustration, and discontent, which may erupt in some form of negative behavior.

The previous discussion may help parents understand better the source of their teen-ager's anger and rebelliousness.

Of equal consideration are the natural biological and emotional stages that adolescents go through. The two qualities—societal and physiological—combine to create a period of what some psychologists see as a time of storm and stress.

Adolescence begins at pubescence with its rapid physical growth, maturation of reproductive functioning, and development of primary and secondary sexual characteristics. The entire process proceeds from pubescence through the end of puberty by which time the maturation and reproductive stages are complete and the individual is sexually able to reproduce. In many non-Western cultures, it is at this point that the child becomes an adult. Most Western societies, however, have put adolescence into the previously mentioned "holding pattern," which extends far past the end of puberty.

The period of adolescence can be divided into two categories: (1) early adolescence, ages twelve to fifteen, and (2) late adolescence, ages sixteen to twenty-one. A major task of both periods of adolescence is the formation of a separate identity. The adolescent must establish an independent identity from that of his or her parents. In early adolescence, teen-agers achieve a more masculine or feminine role. They have a constant drive to accomplish emotional independence from parents and other adults. They also experience a need to become economically independent from their parents. This need for independence, however, is coupled with a contradictory desire to remain in the comfort and security of the role of dependent child. It is, therefore, characteristic for young teen-agers to fluctuate between dependence and independence. This fluctuation can seem to parents like a constant battle that frequently leads to one family crisis or conflict after another.

As the period of adolescence lengthens, the teen-ager frequently becomes resigned to the fact of his or her economic dependence.

In late adolescence, individuals begin selecting vocations and preparing for marriage and family life. At the end of the adolescent period, adolescents should feel prepared to go out and function independently in society. It's interesting to note that adolescents will often move back in with their parents at their first encounter with life's difficulties, then move back out again at a later date.

In addition to the unnaturally prolonged dependence upon parents and the profound physiological and emotional changes that accompany the natural stages of development, adolescents must also contend with peer pressure. It is important to almost all teen-agers to be a part of organizations or groups. The customs and mores of these peer groups can frequently dictate a way of life for them that is more demanding and restrictive than that required by the adolescents' parents. The pressures that adolescents encounter from parents, school authorities, physical changes in their body, and their peer group may often impel them to experiment with drugs and/or alcohol. This experimentation may be an attempt to cope with demands that are beyond their capacity to handle.

Parents should be aware that there are many productive aspects to the stage of development called adolescence: energy, drive, vitality, willingness to work, willingness to take an active role in society, flexibility, readiness to adapt to change, openness, honesty, a strong sense of fairness, and a dislike for intolerance. Most important of all, parents must keep in mind that throughout this period the adolescent is engaged in a sincere and ongoing search for his or her *identity*—even though the methods chosen for achieving this are not always agreeable to adults.

The Adolescent in the Stepfamily

As stated earlier, the stepparent/stepchild relationship is particularly difficult when the stepchild is actually an adolescent. In addition to the rebellious attitude toward parental control that attends the natural stages of development in adolescence, teen-agers in stepfamilies oftentimes have feelings of jealousy and hostility toward their new stepparents. These feelings are compounded by two factors: (1) Adolescent stepchildren have usually spent a good deal of time in the single-parent family in which they may have had a long-standing role of increased independence—a natural consequence of the added responsibility that single-parent family situations create; and (2) in cases where remarriage occurs shortly after the divorce, adolescents may retain vivid memories of both parents and their methods of parental control, or lack of control, in the previous family system.

Feelings of jealousy, hostility, and confusion are usually very normal for adolescents in either of these two situations. In both family systems, adolescents may have been given freedoms and responsibilities of which the new stepparent is unaware. In many single-parent families, the eldest child—in this case the adolescent—is frequently given increased freedom. This is especially true when the adolescent has been elevated to a parent-level position formerly occupied by the absentee parent. In addition to parenting the other children in the family, these adolescents often find that they have more power than the frequently absent custodial parent. In these families, it is not hard to see why adolescents meet stepparents with hostility. To them, the new stepparent may look like an enemy who is trying to usurp their position in the family.

> Joe is widowed with three children—Mike, ten; Karen, twelve; and Sue, seventeen—and recently remarried. Before Joe remarried, Sue was elevated to the role of parent and part-time mother mainly because Joe worked two jobs. Sue became so involved in doing the day-to-day household chores and taking care of her brother and sister that she began to miss school and eventually dropped out. Joe objected at first but later went along with the decision.
>
> Although Joe had dated his new spouse, Joyce, for about six months before they married, the children had spent little time with her. When Joe announced the upcoming marriage, the children all seemed to be fairly agreeable and happy. However, when Joyce arrived on the scene and began taking over many of the duties that Sue had previously been responsible for, a silent war broke out between them. Joyce insisted that Sue return to school and behave like a teen-ager again. The younger children really enjoyed the new family structure; but Sue, unable to adjust, ran away.

The best approach stepparents can take in either situation mentioned is to get involved whenever possible in the family relationships before the marriage. Needless to say, their position will change drastically as they become bona fide members of the new stepfamily. If stepparents take the time to get to know these adolescents before entering into the steprelationship—finding out likes, dislikes, and interests both outside and inside the family—then the chance for a successful relationship is greatly increased. It is important to gain a common ground on which to communicate; it may be foolish to go in loaded with ideas on how to parent the teen-ager.

Stepparents who must raise teen-agers need to proceed

carefully. They may wish to try to establish a one-to-one relationship with the stepadolescent—almost a one-adult-to-another relationship. They may also wish to research adolescent development by reading a good source book or by discussing adolescence with knowledgeable friends. These two precautions will usually help stepparents who have had no experience parenting teen-agers achieve a better relationship with their stepadolescent.

One of the more common complaints of parents in step- and original families is the way adolescents speak or answer back in a "smart tone." Usually, no parent or new stepparent can accept being addressed in a tone of disrespect.

One adolescent's stepmother described her frustration:

> "My teen-age stepson, age fifteen, lives with us, and it sometimes seems like one battle after another. He's been with us for a year now, and we're slowly getting to know one another better, but it's not easy. His father and I insist on knowing *where* he's going when he leaves the house, *who* he's going with, and *when* he'll be back. After several battles over this when he came to live with us, we've finally gotten through to him that it's because we care that we insist on knowing. But, his tone of voice most of the time . . . it really gets to me. He announces where he's off to and who he's going with in the most surly, insolent tone you can imagine. Then we usually end up negotiating his curfew in loud voices. I'll be glad when he's older . . ."

If parents assert themselves and establish early a relationship with their children that emphasizes mutual respect, chances are that this situation will be encountered fewer times than is usual.

By establishing their expectations early, parents communicate to the adolescent that respect is a reciprocal thing. "Respect me and I'll respect you." This is not adult to child—but adult to adult. What adolescents may want is their own identity far removed from that of a child's identity—to be seen and respected as an independent young adult.

Pitfalls to Avoid

It is important for parents and stepparents to develop good listening skills. They must try not to react to the immediate surface statement; they must attempt instead to understand what was behind it. Become an active listener. Refrain, if possible, from coloring what is seen and heard with personal value judgments.

Stepparents who rush in and attempt to force their own values on adolescent stepchildren are usually creating problems immediately. Values are personal to individuals and to families. Trying to force new values on adolescents can be disastrous, for both the adolescent and the stepparent.

Stepparents who rush in to parent and love adolescents who aren't ready to accept that parenting and love are almost assured of failure. There are cases in which the new stepparent wants to make up for whatever pain and suffering the stepchildren may have experienced through divorce or the death of a parent. However, if the teen-ager doesn't want to be immediately parented, stepparents should not force the issue. Instead, stepparents may choose to be supportive and respectful as one adult to another. This careful consideration will allow the relationship the space it needs to develop naturally.

Many natural parents expect new stepparents to take an active role in parenting the children—adolescents included. They are, in fact, depending upon the new stepparent to solve behavior or discipline problems. This expectation on the part of the natural parent must be discussed openly before the remarriage. Many families may choose to hold family meetings to air conflicts and explore members' expectations—what the stepparents' role in discipline will be, what the adolescents want the stepparents' role to be. It must be clear to all family members that the stepparent is not trying to fill the shoes of the absentee parent and that, for the stepparent, the marriage to the children's parent is the first priority. If adolescents can accept this and see that the stepparent's role in relationship to them is not one of an authoritarian but one of an adult who will accept them as equals if respect is reciprocal, a healthier and happier family relationship is likely to be achieved.

If these pitfalls can be avoided, stepparents may find themselves parenting more often than expected. When an adolescent feels that a stepparent is really listening as one adult to another, this adolescent will feel comfortable enough to confide in the stepparent. This confidence and mutual respect may be the start of a comfortable stepparent/stepadolescent relationship.

Guidelines for Stepparents of Adolescents

1. *Be adaptive.* The adolescent has had a history of parenting for many years prior to your arrival on the scene. Explore with your spouse what that previous parenting involved. By incorporating that parenting history into the present framework, stepparent and parent can ease the transition and avoid unnecessary conflict.

2. *Get to know the adolescent before the remarriage.* Take advantage of all opportunities to become acquainted so that both you and the adolescent can form accurate perceptions of one another's strengths and weaknesses. Share time alone together away from the natural parent so that both of you can act naturally without any feeling of being "under observation." (The natural parent may be so anxious for the stepparent-to-be and the adolescent to get along that he or she, inadvertently, applies pressure.)

3. *Understand adolescent development.* Use all available sources of information to more clearly understand adolescence (remember your own adolescence, any previous parenting experience with adolescents, talk with your spouse, friends, professionals, read a textbook on the adolescent life cycle).

4. *Treat the adolescent in an adult-to-adult fashion.* Talk to the teen-ager in an open and straightforward manner on a one-to-one basis.

5. *Cultivate a sense of humor.* Humor can keep the sometimes inexplicable or strange behavior of the adolescent in perspective. Be willing to laugh *together* at the ups and downs of living with each other.

6. *Arrange some privacy for the adolescent.* Most teen-agers need and want privacy, time, and a place to be alone

away from family members. This privacy, however, needs to be balanced with time with the family. Parents often misconstrue the teen-ager's desire for privacy to mean that he or she wants *no* family contact; this is, in most cases, a mistaken assumption because teen-agers do need and want to participate as members of their stepfamilies.

7. *Be positive.* Avoid preaching or criticizing unnecessarily. A common mistake stepparents and natural parents make in light of a teen-ager's perceived fault or mistake is to embark upon a lengthy sermon detailing the problem. This lengthy sermon, no doubt, has been heard before and falls on deaf ears. If constructive criticism is necessary, be brief and to the point in a positive manner.

8. *Clearly differentiate between parenting and discipline.* Parenting and discipline are two separate things. Parenting is how you raise the children; discipline is only a part of that method. Don't present yourself primarily as a disciplinarian. Present yourself as a positive adult figure in the adolescent's life.

VII
The Natural Parent

The role of the natural parent, the parent who has full-time custody of his or her children, is frequently overlooked or dismissed as the "easy job." This chapter will focus on the natural parent in the stepfamily, because this role, too, may be very demanding.

Some natural parents find it difficult to deal with feelings of guilt. They feel guilty, perhaps, that they were unable to prevent the breakup of the original family and worry about the possible harm done to their children. Having "failed" once, the natural parent often feels pressured by self and others to be successful in the second marriage.

A necessary but possibly difficult task for natural parents is the dissolution of the single-parent family system that they so carefully organized after their divorce or the death of their first spouse. It sometimes arouses contradictory feelings of willingness and reluctance. On the one hand, the natural parent may have a desire for the stepparent to take an active role in parenting; she or he is willing to share control. Yet, sometimes the natural parent may feel unsure about the stepparents' role and feel reluctant about relinquishing sole control.

In some stepfamilies, the natural parent's reluctance to share parenting may arise out of a sense of pride in accomplishment as a single parent. It may also, however, arise from a fear that the stepparent may somehow upset the family balance because the stepparent hasn't shared the family's past experiences. Natural parents often feel that they are "on trial." Frequently, natural parents feel like they are being watched and judged by the absentee parent who is waiting outside the family circle with questions like, "Are you doing a good job raising my children?" "Is your home better for the children than mine?" Natural parents are not allowed to make any mistakes; they are expected to be perfect.

Natural parents occupy a central position in the stepfamily system. They are being pulled in a number of directions. They must successfully balance demands from children, spouse, ex-spouse, and relatives; and, in spite of all these demands, they must—for their own sakes—consider their own needs.

Natural parents must balance their children's questions. The children may look to their natural parent for the answers to: Why the divorce? Why the remarriage? What does all this mean for us? Do we have to obey this new stepparent?

In many stepfamilies and single-parent families, the natural parent has neglected to really discuss with or explain to the children the reasons for the divorce. The children have been left with guesses and assumptions. Nor has the natural parent really discussed the meaning of the remarriage for the children—why the natural parent is remarrying and what the new family will, hopefully, be like.

Natural parents must also balance time—time for their new marriage and time for their new stepfamily. Natural parents are oftentimes caught in the middle; their new spouses need time to be alone with them and yet their children need a great deal of their time as they try to adjust to the new family system. Many natural parents lament that they are caught in the middle.

"I feel pulled in two directions," Nancy, a remarried mother of four, explained. "I really feel anxious about my remarriage and about my children. Dan and I need to be alone, to spend time together—we've only been married for eleven months. Yet, my children need me,

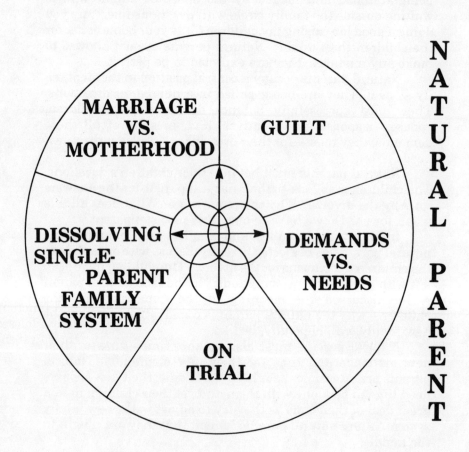

MARRIAGE
VS.
MOTHERHOOD

GUILT

DISSOLVING
SINGLE-
PARENT
FAMILY
SYSTEM

DEMANDS
VS.
NEEDS

ON
TRIAL

NATURAL PARENT

too; they're trying very hard to get used to all the changes—Dan, the house, their new school. When we are all together in the evening, I get pretty nervous. I really want everyone to get along well, so I'm always on edge about it. I find myself running interference between the children and Dan, trying to prevent the children from bugging him. Then I turn around and try to shelter the children from anything Dan may do or say that I know they won't like."

This harried natural parent found herself hovering between husband and children. Because of her anxious need to make sure that everything went smoothly, Nancy found herself unable to relax. She tiptoed around, fearful of any behavior that could be construed as "not getting along." Fortunately for Nancy, Dan and the children were able to see the situation in perspective. They finally had to assure and reassure Nancy that it was okay for all of them to quarrel occasionally or "agree to disagree." After all, they were six separate personalities living together.

"It was hard for Nancy to feel comfortable. She tried so hard to make sure we were all happy. I couldn't seem to convince her that I really like her four children. Oh sure, sometimes they get on my nerves, but the children and I can handle it. I'm sure there are times when I bother them too. What we're doing now is meeting once a week as a family to air our gripes and concerns. That way, we make sure everyone has a chance to have their say, and we're able to prevent any minor problems from becoming major ones. Nancy now feels reassured that we're going to make it as a family."

Another difficulty that natural parents find themselves facing concerns money. Many natural parents find it increasingly difficult to reconcile the amount of child support received monthly with the cost of raising children. The reality for some stepfamilies is that stepparents end up bearing the brunt of the child-rearing expenses. In these situations, either the stepparent or both the stepparent and natural parent work to support the families. In many of these situations, the natural parent may experience harassment from the ex-spouse. This harassment may take the form of a continuing hassle over money: when the child support is sent, how it is used, extras needed by the children.

There is no easy answer to this money riddle. Some stepfamilies choose to pool all financial resources to use for the family as one, while other stepfamilies choose to separate resources to varying degrees. These latter families may choose to maintain separate incomes, sharing living expenses but keeping personal income and child support income separate.

Guidelines for the Natural Parent

1. *Prioritize your time.* Avoid that being-pulled-in-all-directions feeling by prioritizing your time. All natural parents must set aside time for self, time for spouse and marriage, time for children and family. Natural parents must be willing to confront their families with a request for cooperation. "I want to be able to spend time with all of you, but I will need you to help me by taking turns..."

2. *Be present and future oriented.* Avoid dwelling on the past; focus instead on the present. Devote your energies to making the present the best possible for you and your family. Retrain yourself, if necessary, to notice at least *one* positive quality or behavior concerning your spouse and children (all individually, of course). Positively reinforce that quality or behavior you admire by the use of praise, a smile, a hug, a thank-you, an appreciative remark, a reward, or some other appropriate gesture or reinforcer.

3. *Be yourself.* Ignore that feeling of being on trial and concentrate on being yourself. No one can be perfect all of the time. Natural parents must have the ego strength to act as they see fit as a parent, regardless of the judgmental attitudes of others.

4. *Be willing to risk.* The task of dissolving the single-parent family system—usually a comfortable, known way of

life—can seem risky. The stepfamily and its shared parenting responsibilities is an unknown factor at first, but any reluctance or unwillingness to commit oneself 100 percent to the creation of a cohesive stepfamily—an unwillingness to parent together as a team of natural parent/stepparent—may ultimately result in estrangement between spouses and the possible breakdown of the new stepfamily.

5. *Be willing to set limits*. Natural parents remarry for their own needs, not the needs of the children. The remarriage comes first. This does not mean that natural parents love their children less; it means that they recognize their priorities. If the natural parent is happy and fulfilled in the second marriage, then the chances are increased that the natural parent will be happier and more successful as a parent.

6. *Relax*. Don't feel that you must run interference between spouse and children. Natural parents cannot serve as the buffer in the stepfamily for more than a brief period of time. Stepparents and stepchildren need to be allowed the opportunity to develop a comfortable relationship together; they need to experience opportunities to learn to accommodate and adjust to one another.

VIII
Absentee Parent

Previous chapters have focused on the roles of immediate family members in an attempt to create a model for members of a stepfamily. In the immediate stepfamily, each member has a place in the family and the opportunity to grow and develop stepfamily relationships.

The absentee parent has a place in the family also and must have the opportunity, if possible, to maintain the family relationship with the children. Many absentee parents complain of feeling like outsiders; the reality for most absentee parents is that they play a diminished role in their children's lives after the divorce.

This diminished role does not mean that absentee parents are less of a parent nor does it mean they no longer deserve the respect and obedience of their children. The diminished role does mean that maintaining a strong parental relationship with the children requires an enormous amount of hard work. Many absentee parents fall into the role of older friend or pal.

Success in maintaining a strong parent/child relationship can be attributed to one important consideration: consistency. Absentee parents must be consistent in their contacts with their children and consistent in their dealings with their ex-spouse. Absentee parents must consistently schedule visits with their children, follow through absolutely on these visits and plans, and involve themselves as much as possible in their children's lives.

This involvement can be facilitated by continuing and maintaining the structure set up by the single-parent family or stepfamily. Whenever possible, absentee parents can maintain family rules, family traditions, and ways of doing things as similar as possible to their counterparts in parenting—their ex-spouse. This cooperation and continuity between absentee parent and custodial parent can be one of the most crucial necessities to a successful partnership in parenting between the two.

Failure on the part of the absentee parent to provide this continuity between the custodial parent's house and the absentee parent's house usually results in an uncomfortable adjustment for the children as they move between the two homes. Absentee parents may find it difficult to carry out this continuity for several reasons. One, many absentee parents feel guilty that they cannot spend more time with their children and, so, succumb to the temptation to make every visit a Disneyland. Two, some absentee parents find it impossible to cooperate in any way with their ex-spouses and refuse to reinforce the custodial parent's efforts to provide structure for the children. Third, some absentee parents worry or fear that the stepparent is taking their place and try to "outshine" the stepparent by extravagant gestures.

Many absentee parents' efforts to maintain strong ties to their children are well-intentioned with upsetting results.

Brian is a twenty-eight-year-old divorced father of a four-year-old girl, Susie. He is bitter over the divorce, over losing custody of his little girl, and over his ex-wife's remarriage. Brian wants very much to play a more active role in his daughter's life and fights against losing her affection to her new stepfather. Brian lives alone in a small, spartan apartment, but before he picks up his daughter, he transforms it into a wonderland by placing 150 brightly colored, stuffed animals around the two rooms. The weekend is packed with outings, treats, and late nights.

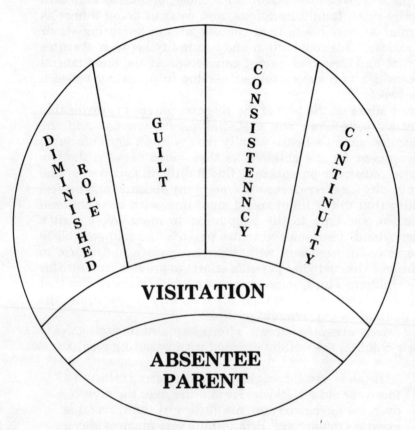

Brian does not discipline Susie; he fears that any attempts at discipline will spoil their weekend together. On Sunday nights, Brian returns Susie to her mother and the difficulties start. Obviously, a four-year-old child will prefer the immediate pleasures of weekend wonderland to the longer lasting benefits of weekday daily living with all its structure.

At first, Susie's mother and stepfather felt helpless to deal with Brian's extravagance. Eventually, the helplessness turned into anger, and open conflict broke out between Susie's natural parents. The child became a pawn in a custody struggle between them.

Why do so many absentee parents act like Brian or in a manner similar to his? In Brian's case, he was focusing on what he had lost rather than seeking to build a new life for himself in which his daughter could play a part.

If absentee parents fail to become reconciled to their diminished role in their children's lives and fail to build new lives for themselves, they will often sabotage their ex-spouse's efforts to provide a stable family life for the children. Once absentee parents are comfortable in their situations, however, they tend to cooperate more fully with the parent with custody. Visits are more natural, less of a wonderland, and more in line with the structure of the children's full-time home.

This is to the advantage of both absentee parent and the children. The children notice the consistency, respect, and cooperation between parents. It emphasizes that parents remain parents, concerned for their children's welfare regardless of divorce. It eliminates the questions or insinuations between ex-spouses that usually puts the children uncomfortably in the middle. The cooperation ensures that the children will be able to enjoy time spent with the absentee parent and with the parent with custody free of recriminations or lamentation over the past.

If absentee parents are really interested in the welfare of their children, they will do what they can to enhance the relationships between themselves, their children, and their ex-spouse. The benefits of this cooperation for the absentee

parent are worthwhile: Ex-spouses are usually more apt to
recognize the importance of the absentee parent's role in their
children's lives and assist him or her in maintaining strong
relationships by effecting a good working relationship. The
absentee parent and the ex-spouse can make it possible for each
other to have both quality time as parents and time alone with
their respective partners to enhance their personal relationships.

Guidelines for the Absentee Parent

1. *Make sure your children can count on you.* Visits should
be regular, and you should be on time for each one. Absentee
parents can be unintentionally cruel by being late. Many
children, anxious and eager to see their absentee parent, are
ready and waiting hours before the scheduled time of arrival.
When the absentee parent does not show up on time, the
children spend agonizing minutes or hours worrying whether
or not their parent will show up.

2. *Be flexible.* As the children grow older, their time
becomes crowded with school activities and friends. They may
feel reluctant to drop these interests every other weekend and
go to visit their absentee parent. Yet, they may be fearful of
hurting their parent's feelings. Absentee parents can be
flexible by becoming involved in any of their children's
activities that they can share, or by showing a willingness to
schedule their time together around some of these activities.

3. *Be firm.* Some absentee parents complain of feeling like
a walking checkbook. Many absentee parents want to make up
for their inability to spend more time with their children. They
try to make it up to the children by substituting money and
gifts. They also allow themselves to be manipulated by the
children and ex-spouse into giving even more and more. As the
demands or expectations escalate, absentee parents may begin
to feel that they must continue to give and give or risk losing
their children's love or ex-spouse's cooperation. Avoid this
vicious circle by firmly stating what your limits are regarding
those "extras."

4. *Be creative.* Quantity of time is not as important as the quality of that time. Quality time is time spent *together*. It need not be an outing or a special event. It may be time spent doing simple things together like watching television, gardening, working on the car. What is crucial is the communication between parent and child that occurs during the activity. Disneyland can be fun once in a while, but a constant routine of going there does two things: (1) It sets the child up to expect to be entertained, and (2) the hectic pace decreases the opportunity for meaningful communication.

5. *Be considerate.* Absentee parents can provide the opportunity for their relatives—grandparents, aunts, uncles, and cousins—to maintain contact with their children. They have a responsibility, though, to ensure that extended family members do not try to sabotage the custodial parent's structure. In other words, absentee parents need to consider "briefing" their relatives. They need to encourage the relatives to support and promote cooperation between family members.

IX
The Stepfamily Diagram

A useful tool for stepfamilies in their efforts to define and clarify roles is the stepfamily diagram. This diagram is simply a picture that helps members *see* the interrelationships and power balances between family members inside and outside the family circle.

Its usefulness lies also in the fact that diagraming a picture of the family gives members a visible framework around which to orient a discussion. Can you picture a parent and stepparent gathering together with the children and saying, "Okay, children, we are now going to define and clarify our roles in our stepfamily." Of course not. The children would warily eye the adults and think, "They've gone nuts!"

More naturally a parent and stepparent could pass around large sheets of paper and a variety of colored pencils and felt-tip markers to all members of the family as they finish dinner, or, are gathered in front of the television. They may prefer to say something like, "Okay, we're each going to draw a picture of what our family looks like—who's in it, and who's in charge, and how we all fit together."

Some guidelines for the family drawing are as follows:

The diagram has three major parts

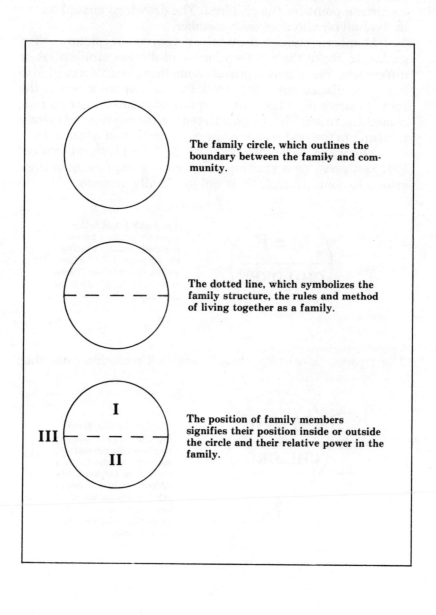

The family circle, which outlines the boundary between the family and community.

The dotted line, which symbolizes the family structure, the rules and method of living together as a family.

The position of family members signifies their position inside or outside the circle and their relative power in the family.

Parents should encourage children to draw their own pictures—to express their own idea of how they see the family. The parent may or may not wish to explain the family circle as a starting point for the children. The drawings should be the individual creations of each member.

Members should draw their individual picture, then gather to share their perceptions and discuss similarities or differences. The pictures provide something *visible* on which to hang the discussion. They are a tool to help members of the family clarify their thoughts and provide something concrete, something to see. They are not the end in themselves but merely a means to the end result: clear communication about roles.

There is a basic stereotype of the "ideal natural family" that can serve as a starting point for the stepfamily in their efforts to conceptualize their unique family system.

The mother and father together are in a power position, equally sharing the responsibility for parenting the children. There is little or no intrusion on the family's boundaries.

The typical "ideal stepfamily" may look something like this:

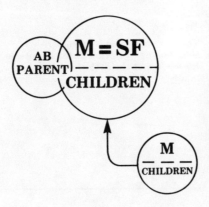

Mother and stepfather together are the power position, equally parenting mother's children who live with them full time. Stepfather's children visit every other weekend. Both parents have a cooperative parenting relationship with their ex-spouse.

Of course, the ideal and the reality are often strikingly different. How one would like things to be and how they actually are may be very far apart. In this process of diagraming, the stepfamily members may want to draw two separate family pictures: (1) the reality of things; (2) the ideal toward which they would like to work.

The following are some actual examples of family diagrams as drawn by stepfamily members.

Table 1: In this family diagram drawn by a fifteen-year-old girl, there are four adults who seem to play somewhat equal roles in parenting the children (Example 1). This teen-ager did not define her family in terms of "Mom's house" and "Dad's house" by drawing two family circles. She instead said all of these people are my family; all four adults are important to me. Her stepmother initially felt slighted (Example 2) by her stepdaughter's perception. The girl had put all four adults in her life—her mother, her mother's boyfriend, her father, and her stepmother—on an equal level.

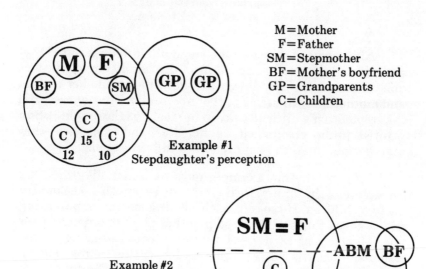

M = Mother
F = Father
SM = Stepmother
BF = Mother's boyfriend
GP = Grandparents
C = Children

Example #1
Stepdaughter's perception

Example #2
As stepmother would have
liked the diagram: her
"ideal" perception

M = Mother
F = Father
SM = Stepmother
BF = Mother's boyfriend
GP = Grandparents
C = Children

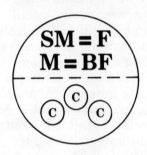

Example #3
The "real" perception
stepmother and stepdaughter
agreed to work toward.

After some discussion, the stepmother felt reassured that she was indeed vitally important in the family circle. She was able to accept her stepdaughter's need to include her mother and mother's boyfriend as part of her family. They agreed that the stepmother's difficulty lay in her feelings (Example 3). She wanted to be recognized as her husband's partner—they *together* parented the children on a full-time basis.

Table 2: In this example natural father diagrams his perception of the family. He has custody every other weekend of his two children. He sees himself playing the major parenting role at these times with the stepmother playing a much lesser role. He recognizes a need for more equal sharing of the responsibility. His wife's perception echoes this feeling of being on the "outside," not sharing an equal position. The daughter's diagram shows her desire for "Mom and Dad back together again" but also recognizes the reality of the divorce and remarriage. By discussing these perceptions, all three were able to understand each other's perception better. Redefining roles, the father made the effort to dissolve the single-parent family system he had been maintaining and include his new wife as a partner in his dealings with the children.

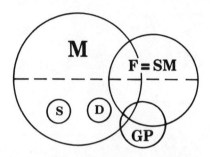

Father's perception of reality
on weekends

Father's perception of
ideal on weekends

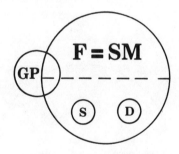

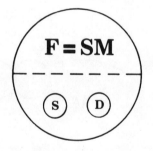

Father's perception of reality
on weekdays

Father's perception of ideal
on weekdays

M = Mom
S = Son
D = Daughter
GP = Grandparent

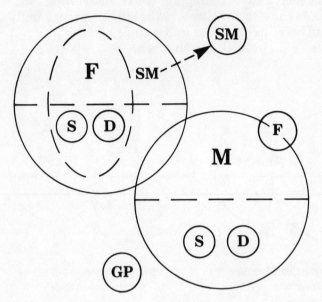

Stepmother's perception of reality on weekdays

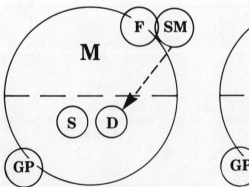

Stepmother's perception of ideal
on weekdays

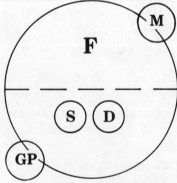

Stepmother's perception of
reality on weekends

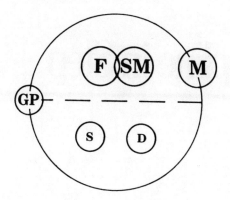

Stepmother's perception of
the ideal on the weekend

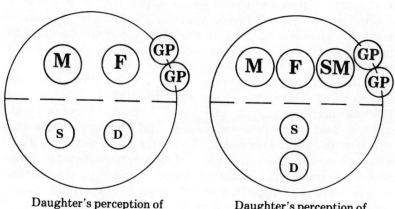

Daughter's perception of   Daughter's perception of
the ideal situation   the reality

Drawing a diagram of the family can be a useful catalyst
to discovery. Members can explore how they see their
relationships to one another and open the door to more
comfortable steprelating.

X
Discipline in Step

A constant concern of parents in a steprelationship is that of discipline. How much are stepparents expected to discipline? Do they want to discipline someone else's children? Are they, in fact, parents or just people who happen to have married parents? How do stepparents get the stepchildren to follow the rules and structure of the house? If they use discipline, will their spouse run to the rescue of the stepchildren?

As pointed out in previous chapters, parents—both natural and step—deserve respect and obedience from the children and should receive it. Deserving it and receiving it are two different matters, however. Most stepparents want to be parents in more than name only; they want to play an active role in helping to raise the stepchildren in their home. Some rush in eager to parent; some play a waiting game. Almost all make mistakes when it comes to discipline.

One of the most common mistakes can be described as follows:

Ed and Pam have been married for one year. Pam's four-year-old daughter lives with them all of the time; Ed's two eight- and ten-year-old sons visit every weekend. Ed and Pam have a problem.

122

Pam is very proud of her beautiful home and keeps it meticulously clean. On Fridays, Pam's daughter leaves to visit her father, and Ed's two sons arrive to visit for the weekend. Ed's sons are very active, boisterous boys whose favorite activity at their father's house is to build forts out of the white sofa cushions. The mess they make infuriates Pam. She becomes even angrier when their father doesn't seem affected by the boys' destructive activities, but she doesn't say anything to the boys or her husband. On the other hand, Ed dislikes Pam's daughter's attitude toward him. Once, when he went into her room at night, she said, "Don't you come in my room! You're not my father..." All he could think of to say was, "Goodnight."

On Sunday evening when the boys depart and the little girl is sleeping, Ed and Pam begin to fight about discipline. Rather than enjoy the peace and quiet alone together, they hurl accusations at one another. "Your two sons are tearing apart the house—you don't even try to keep them in line!" "Well, your daughter is rude and ungrateful—ordering me out of her room! Who pays for that room?"

The argument usually escalated by Monday or Tuesday from fighting as parents to fighting as husband and wife. On Wednesday they made up and on Friday the whole cycle began again. They were successful at arguing but unsuccessful at disciplining each other's children.

The above example, called the "eggshell phenomenon," is a common occurrence in stepfamilies. In this situation, stepparents are afraid to discipline the stepchild because they fear the reaction of their mate. So they walk on eggshells, avoiding disciplining the other's child. They fear both the child's reaction to them as a wicked stepparent and their spouse's reaction. "Hey! You can't tell my child what to do!" Some stepparents are extremely wary of this; they assume that if they can't get along with the children 100 percent of the time, the spouse might leave.

Two factors contribute to the eggshell phenomenon. One, the stepparent has either had no prior experience with disciplining children or has no idea as to how the children have been disciplined in the past; or two, parent and stepparent have not discussed how the children should be disciplined and by whom.

Again, the element of time is crucial. In the original family, mother and father developed their ideas on discipline together over time. In the stepfamily, this time is missing. Before remarriage, the emphasis was on developing the relationship as a couple. Usually, little or no emphasis was placed on disciplining; the children were seen as "no problem." Once married, both spouses feel a need to develop an emphasis on discipline but find themselves "walking on eggshells."

The remedy for the eggshell phenomenon is straightforward. Husband and wife must first sit down *together*, free from distractions, to discuss discipline. It is crucial to the success of the stepfamily to determine at this point whether or not the single-parent family system has been dissolved. Is discipline going to be a joint and equal venture between partners? Or is the natural parent expecting to continue disciplining as previously carried out in the single-parent family—including the new spouse in the disciplining only when it is convenient to do so? If it is going to be a joint venture (as it should be), the natural parent must clearly give the stepparent permission to join in disciplining the children as an equal partner. The two must discuss issues of discipline, sharing their ideas on past experiences and how they view discipline in the stepfamily. Stepparents, especially those who do not have children of their own, can learn a great deal from natural parents. Natural parents can often benefit from the ideas and suggestions of stepparents too. Stepparents have distance—often a clearer perspective—because of the fact of the steprelationship, whereas the natural parent may be too deeply enmeshed with the discipline situation to clearly see all the factors in perspective.

This discussion must be more than a philosophical exercise; spouses need to focus specifically on what is important to them as parents. Many parents have been coached to draw up two lists. One list includes all those specific rules or behaviors that they *as parents* feel are important for the children. These behaviors are not negotiable; these behaviors are a "must." The other list includes all those behaviors or rules that they *as parents* feel are negotiable, that the child has some freedom of choice within certain limits. For the young child, the list of nonnegotiables is often long. As the child matures, the list becomes shorter. Each parent in the stepfamily has his or her own lists. These lists must be shared and blended together, prioritizing from most important to least important.

Some parents and stepparents may choose to begin with the following checklist as an aid to clarifying thoughts on discipline. Each should complete the checklist separately, then compare together their individual responses. This is only meant as a catalyst to ideas, not as an all-inclusive list. Parents may choose to elaborate and expand the list.

Rate the following behaviors on the continuum:

NEGOTIABLE	NON NEGOTIABLE
(Child has some choice in the decision making.)	(Child has no say in the decision making. Parents have full control.)
a. School attendance	l. Use of money earned independently
b. School grades	m. Drinking
c. Homework	n. Drugs
d. Home chores	o. Smoking
e. Manners	p. Privacy
f. Dress	q. Curfew
g. Dating habits (what and how)	r. Sex
h. Bedtime	s. "attitude" toward family members (manners, tone of voice, gestures, participation in family activities)
i. Choice of friends	
j. Where allowed to go	
k. Use of allowance	t. "Attitude" toward extended family members
	u. Others

The following lists were drawn up by the parent and stepparent of two fourteen-year-old twin girls; they had separate lists for their two younger children.

NONNEGOTIABLE
1. Attend family meeting every Sunday from 6:00 to 7:00 P.M.
2. Three W's: Where you're going, who you're going with, when you'll be home.
3. Attend school every day, all classes.
4. Earn all passing grades (C or better).
5. One hour homework, Sunday through Thursday.
6. No drugs or alcohol.

NEGOTIABLE
1. Home chores chosen and rotated monthly among children.
2. Dress—clothing allowance given monthly. Choice of purchases and what to wear up to each teen-ager.
3. Friendships—parents place confidence in their daughters' ability to choose their own friends.
4. Privacy—daughters allowed to spend time in their rooms without recriminations; their rooms are their private domain.
5. Any money earned independently may be spent independently.

Once these two lists of negotiable and nonnegotiable behaviors have been agreed upon, parent and stepparent present the guidelines to the children. It is important that the children hear this from both parent and stepparent together. They must view the two as a united unit. It is probable that the children will test to see if the natural parent really means to back the stepparent up 100 percent.

This can be especially important in the case of those stepparents who care for their stepchildren full time. The children need to know that the stepparent has the natural parent's full permission to discipline and that he or she backs the stepparent up 100 percent.

Possibly, the natural parents may find themselves in disagreement with a particular action taken by the stepparent in an effort to discipline. If that happens, it is crucial that the natural parent support the stepparent in front of the children. Then, in private, parent and stepparent can discuss the issue and come to an agreement. They can discuss this agreement with the children—the end result is that parent and stepparent have not underminded each other's efforts nor taken sides with the children against the spouse. The message comes from both parent and stepparent.

Guidelines on Discipline

1. *Be specific.* Give children a clear, precise, and very specific direction on the nonnegotiable items. No commercials or persuasions are necessary. For example, the parent and stepparent in the previous example might say, "On Sundays from 6:00 to 7:00 P.M., we expect you both to join our family meeting. That means that you will schedule all other activities around this. The purpose of our family meetings will be to air concerns, give everyone a chance to have his or her 'say,' and plan together as a family."

2. *Be prepared.* Be prepared to follow through—to let the children know that you really mean what you say. Follow-through and consistency are perhaps the *most* important ingredients to success in discipline. If parents say, "Okay, these few things are not negotiable," and then fail to really mean it—the result is disastrous. For example, in the situation just described, the parent and stepparent must be prepared to say no to the first request to skip the family meeting.

3. *Discuss discipline early in the relationship.* Discipline is only a part of parenting; it is not parenting in its entirety. Discipline is, however, an important task in defining parent and stepparent roles. Parents and stepparents may wish to ask themselves and each other, "What is my (our) philosophy on discipline? Do I (we) feel that physical punishment is effective? Are our decisions realistic considering the age and maturity of each child? Am I (are we) willing to insist and follow through

on the non-negotiable behaviors as a team?" Again, the
checklist may help serve as a catalyst to discussion; it is not
intended to be a solution.

Disciplining the Adolescent

Disciplining the adolescent is somewhat different from
disciplining preteen-agers and young children; and, therefore,
it needs to be discussed here to prevent confusion.

Many parents, both step and natural, feel that disciplining the adolescent is an exercise in futility. One of the most
common reasons is that parents find the former methods of
discipline, which sometimes included physical punishment, to
be no longer effective. The child has grown up, and it seems that
he or she is no longer afraid of the consequences of not doing
what parents expect. Oftentimes, it seems like the parent has
lost control overnight.

In confusion over the fact that the old tried and true ways
aren't effective anymore, parents often try to incorporate a
variety of new techniques. They may use the fear of restriction,
bargaining, or, when all else fails, a series of shouting matches
that never seem to end. Some parents throw their arms in the
air in surrender—it's an impossible stage and nothing works.
Most parents, however, hold to the belief that they will be
successful, although they are constantly looking for an easier
and more successful way of interacting with their adolescent
children.

For stepparents who have never had children of their own,
the question is often, "How am I supposed to discipline a child
who I am having difficulty parenting?" We would suggest
taking a second look at the chapter dealing with stepchildren,
paying particular attention to that portion concerned with the
adolescent stepchild.

In addition, Harold F. Zuckerman in his book *Adolescence
Is a Required Course* offers the following guidelines for dealing
with adolescents:*

1. *Don't discount.* Value what is said by the adolescent,
and allow him to be wrong. If he tells you that he is angry about
something, acknowledge that he is angry; do not tell him not to

---

*Harold F. Zuckerman. *Adolescence Is a Required Course.* (Morristown, N.J.: General Learning
Press/Silver Burdett Company, 1976). Copyright © General Learning Press. Reprinted by Permission.

be. When he asks a rational question, such as, "Why are we doing this?" give a straight answer that shows respect for his thinking rather than putting him down for asking.

2. *Be open and honest with your feelings and emotions.* It is okay to say, for example, "I'm angry about *what you did.* What are you going to do about it?" This does not make him not okay. You can teach him to express his feelings and emotions and not to hide them. Leave room for disagreement.

3. *Respond literally to what is said.* If a young person says that he has a headache, do not offer an aspirin. If one asks if you have a car, do not offer a ride. If you are asked, "Do you have a pencil?" answer "Yes, I do." Place adolescents in a position of thinking for themselves and saying exactly what they mean.

4. *Be direct and assertive.* Passive teachers and parents ask for trouble. Say what you want or feel. Use "I" messages as opposed to "you" messages. "I want you to clean up your room" is better than "You should clean up your room."

5. *Get adolescents to think as adults.* "Are you willing to do that?" "That is not acceptable behavior." "You have two choices, what do you want to do?" "How will you solve your problem?" Straight and direct questions are the best way to hook the adult in the adolescent.

XI
Planning Together: A Cooperative Responsibility

A stepfamily is a cooperative responsibility. Success requires the cooperation of all members and their commitment to working together to blend as a family. It requires blending family perceptions, resolving any residual issues stemming from the interim period, and defining roles; but the work does not stop with these three tasks.

Successful steprelationships involve planning together: communication, a strong marital relationship, and consideration of legal and financial issues. These areas of the cooperative responsibility will be explored in this chapter.

Communication

Open communication can aptly be described as the key to success in all the other areas of the successful steprelationship. Without effective and honest communication, attempts to resolve the difficulties are doomed to failure.

Communication means both talking and listening, being willing to express one's personal thoughts and feelings, and being willing to hear another's personal thoughts and feelings. It means being able to sustain a conversation through the resolution or compromise without losing one's temper or stalking off in icy silence.

Effective communication is a skill and must be acquired and practiced. The following communication exercises are particularly helpful in acquiring and practicing the skill of communication. Once learned, these exercises become naturally incorporated in one's everyday communication. They are especially helpful to stepfamilies for one simple reason: Communication channels become easily tangled in the stepfamily due to the sheer number of individuals involved and their varied past histories and ways of doing things. There are more opportunities for misunderstandings, hurt feelings, and resentments in the absence of effective communication.

The following three communication skills are presented to help parents and stepparents relearn how to talk and how to listen. They should be practiced as an exercise and then the skills themselves may be incorporated into everyday language.

The first skill is ventilation. Oftentimes, an individual just wants to unwind, let off steam, or rehash a day's events. It is the chance to talk that is wanted, not necessarily the chance to receive advice or hear someone else's opinions. This can be likened to a teapot. Someone lights the burner, the water begins to heat, it begins to boil, and the lid starts rattling. As the pressure builds up, the lid comes dangerously close to blowing off. Someone comes along and turns off the heat, the boiling water in the teapot subsides and eventually cools.

Ventilating works in the same manner. One person has really "had it" and needs a chance to let off steam. Another individual provides this opportunity for ventilating. After the individual has let off steam and is feeling much calmer, the two can begin to discuss resolution of the matter. Sometimes, just ventilating is all that is needed.

VENTILATION:
EXERCISE IN COMMUNICATION

Rules: No eye contact, pair links arms or hands, one listener, one talker, listener can only say "uh huh," "yes," "I'm listening," "I hear you."

Step One: Talker begins ventilating about a current issue, problem, or gripe. Listener interjects one of four allowable responses when talker pauses or as talker talks; listener does this repeatedly while talker talks.

Step Two: When talker winds down, listener asks, "What have you done?"

Step Three: Talker begins to ventilate again about different solutions tried, ideas about what to do, and so forth.

Step Four: When talker winds down again, listener says, "If I were you—but I'm not, so you can disregard this feedback—I would do..." (Listener gives *one* suggestion.)

Step Five: Then talker has a few minutes to ruminate on the suggestion.

The second skill is learning to really listen to what someone is saying and grasping the main ideas being expressed. Frequently, when two people are communicating, they are talking but not listening. While the talker talks, the "listener" is planning what he or she will say next and completely misses the talker's point. The result can be frustrating for both and lead to "You don't understand." Of course, neither understands; neither heard what the other said.

The following two exercises teach individuals to "track one another," or follow closely what the other is saying and summarize the main ideas in a more concise manner.

FEEDBACK I:
EXERCISE IN COMMUNICATION

Object: The object for the talker is to have one's say uninterrupted and learn to regulate the pace of one's utterances. The object for the listener is to learn to digest what is being said and to prove that one is listening.

Rules: Sit opposite each other, establish eye contact, one listener, one talker, listener uses a "time-out" sign.

Step One: Talker begins to talk and tries to regulate him- or herself, pausing at appropriate intervals so listener can feed back.

Step Two: Listener listens until talker has said a few sentences, flashes "time-out" sign if talker doesn't pause, then repeats *word for word* (tranposing pronouns) what the talker said.

Example: "I want you to...," talker.
"You want me to...," listener.

FEEDBACK II:
EXERCISE IN COMMUNICATION

Object: To bring out the best of what the talker is saying; separate the immaterial details from the main point.

Rules: Sit opposite each other, establish eye contact, one listener, one talker, listener uses a "time-out" sign.

Talker: Talker begins to talk and tries to regulate him- or herself, pausing at appropriate intervals so listener can feed back.

Listener: Listener takes the talker's statements and turns them into *elegant* statements, enhances and summarizes the main ideas. He or she may also include a careful interpretation.

Example: *Talker:* "I feel so frustrated when I come home from work, and the children haven't done their chores. Especially the kitchen...the dirty dishes are still piled up from breakfast, and there's usually a mess left from their after-school snacks. I start dinner surrounded by all that mess."
Listener: "When you get home from work, you'd like to have all the children's chores done. You'd like to be able to start dinner in a clean kitchen."
Talker: "Yes, I don't think it's asking too much to

expect the children to have all their chores and homework done by 6:00. John has to get better grades, he never studies. Susie has got the TV going all afternoon. I hate to have to come home and nag at them to get everything done. I wish I could come home and have a few peaceful moments to myself to relax before I start dinner."

Listener: "You feel it's reasonable to expect the children to have chores and homework complete by the time you get gome so that you can relax peacefully for a few minutes before starting to cook dinner."

The third skill involves learning to recognize all the many assumptions we make concerning those around us. Members of a family make assumptions about what other members are thinking or why they behave in a certain way; and they then respond accordingly. For example, a wife notices that her husband has a tense, angry look on his face as he comes in the door after work one evening. She assumes that it is due to the fact that their son left his bicycle and toys in the driveway again. She tiptoes around her husband, avoiding their usual predinner talk because she doesn't want to argue or have to defend their son's carelessness. Yet the assumption is very wrong as they almost always are. The tense, angry look on her husband's face is not due to the bicycle in the driveway. The reason is not even family related; her husband had to endure a rush-hour traffic jam on the freeway, and he is hot and aggravated as a result. However, since he is not aware of his wife's assumption, he does not understand her avoidance of their usual, cozy tête-à-tête. Assuming she's mad at him for something, he withdraws into a puzzled silence.

CHECKING OUT ASSUMPTIONS: EXERCISE IN COMMUNICATION

Object: To verify assumptions made concerning one another.

Rules: Follow the following steps. Choose a talker and a
                listener. Talker focuses on a recent assumption he
                or she wishes to clarify.

Step One: Talker asks listener, "Do I have permission to read
                your mind?"

Step Two: Listener grants permission.

Step Three: Talker says, "Thank you."

Step Four: *Talker:* "My mind-read of you in ____ situation
                (describes situation) is that you felt/thought..."

Step Five: Listener actively listens (summarizes or repeats
                back to talker what talker just said).

Step Six: *Talker:* "Thank you for listening. What portion of
                my mind-read is true?"

Step Seven: Listener gives percentage of truth/falseness.

Step Eight: *Talker:* "Thank you. May I explore what was right
                or wrong?"

Step Nine: Pair discusses what in the mind-read was correct/
                incorrect.

In the foregoing example, the wife may have chosen to read her husband's mind. "Bert, my mind-read of why you looked so angry when you came in the door tonight is that you were angry that Brian left his toys and bicycle in the driveway blocking the garage."

"You thought I was mad because I had to stop and move the bicycle and toys out of the driveway so that I could pull the car into the garage."

"Thank you, what portion of my mind-read was correct?"

"Well, actually none of it. I may have looked angry because of a traffic jam I had to endure in this heat on the commute home from work. I really get tense sitting in all that traffic."

These communication skills become natural with practice. They can be tools to more effective communication in the stepfamily if members choose to use them.

The Couple Bond

In order for a stepfamily to succeed, parent and stepparent must first have a strong, healthy relationship as husband and wife. Their "couple bond" must be firmly cemented to avoid the possibility of family problems or the children driving a wedge between them.

The reality of family living can be very different from the romantic excitement of courtship and dating. The couple needs to have time alone to strengthen its relationship so that together, as a team, it can face the challenges of working out a day-to-day blend of family. A honeymoon, rather than a family vacation, is a must. Weekends alone, away from family pressures, are also a must at least every six weeks. This time alone can be a chance to continue to explore one another and renew the relationship as husband and wife—a couple rather than two parents.

Many stepparents find this prescription for time alone, away from family, difficult to follow. One mother of three teen-agers described her dilemma to a class of fellow stepparents.

> "I just can't leave for a whole weekend. My daughter is dating now and I'm afraid she'd stay out too late if we aren't home. And my two boys...I know they'd sneak the extra car out or, worse yet, throw a wild party at our house."

Her list of fears was endless; her husband had given up trying to talk her into going away for a weekend. Class members began questioning her about her children. It became apparent after a while that the woman's children were, in fact, pretty responsible sixteen-, seventeen-, and eighteen-year-old teen-agers. The daughter was not dating any one boy seriously, and the two sons both worked at jobs that required responsibility and dependability. Nothing that the woman described indicated any reason not to trust them for a weekend.

Under pressure from the group, the woman agreed to try going away for a short trip. Her husband immediately arranged a romantic weekend for two in the mountains nearby. When the class met again, the two reported, "We had a great time... it really was relaxing to be away by ourselves. No children, no phone, no friends in and out. We talked and talked..."

The husband added, "I was really proud of my wife. She only called home twice to reassure herself that all was well; and I was really grateful to the kids for handling themselves responsibly so that their mother could feel comfortable."

Other stepparents and parents find it difficult to manage these weekend trysts financially. One young mother and stepfather described their problem as follows:

> "We're on a really tight budget. There's very little money left over after bills for any extras. We really wanted to get away, but we felt that the cost of hiring a baby-sitter for the weekend was just too high. Neither of us has parents or relatives nearby. Who could take our three kids for a weekend? My husband came up with a really workable solution. We'd become good friends with this other young couple in our stepparenting class. They had the same problem we did, and one night my husband suggested that we help each other out."

> "We arranged to take their two kids for one weekend while they went away. Then, they took our three kids for the next weekend! It worked fine: The kids had a ball, and my husband and I had a wonderfully private weekend for two here at home. Now we've agreed with our friends to trade off one weekend every other month. My husband and I are putting aside $20 each month so that soon we'll be able to go away for our weekend, too."

This time alone can provide the opportunity to develop the warm, intimate relationship vital to a healthy marriage. It can be a reminder to both spouses that they married for each other, not for the children. When individuals feel fulfilled in their relationship as husband and wife, they will be more nurturing, effective parents.

It is important that the children see the affection between parent and stepparent. Open affection can reassure the children that the marriage will last, that they can relax within the security of the new family system.

In a stepfamily in which the stepmother cares full time for the stepchildren, it is especially important to find this special husband/wife time alone. The stepmother in this family situation has a large responsibility for raising the children, yet she married to become a wife not a stepmother. She is especially vulnerable to needing reassurance from her husband that he married her for a wife, not a mother for his children. The weekends alone can be a time for this reassurance and renewal. Of course, the stepmother in this family situation knew when she married that she would be caring for her husband's children. Yet, doubt can be an insidious companion for the stepmother. As she does the daily routine of house and child care, she may find herself wondering, "Where is the romance and excitement of the courtship? Did he marry me out of convenience?"

The husband's responsibility in these situations is to generate and maintain the romance of the husband/wife relationship as a respite from their day-to-day family life. The weekends alone can be the method for achieving this.

Legal Issues

The legal status of the stepparent is often confusing and vague. It is aptly described by several authors as "obligations without rights." Laws concerning stepfamilies are written to the disadvantage of the stepparent; they focus on protecting rights of natural parents and protecting society from financial burden.

One clear fact emerges from the confusion. There is no legal relationship between stepparent and stepchild just because the stepparent marries the child's natural parent. For example, the stepparent is in a very weak position in a struggle for custody. After a divorce or in the case of the death of the natural parent, the stepparent has none of the customary visitation privileges that are the right of the noncustody parent. This lack of visitation rights may be devastating to a stepparent who has raised a stepchild for a number of years.

> Jerry was divorced by his wife after eleven years of marriage. He and his thirteen-year-old stepdaughter were very close. Although her natural father lived only fifty miles away, she had seen him only twice in thirteen years. Since the divorce, his ex-wife had taken her daughter and moved to another county. She refused to let him visit his stepdaughter despite the pleas of both daughter and ex-husband. To make matters worse, the girl was very unhappy in her new environment where her mother's alcoholic boyfriend had moved in. She desperately wanted to live with her stepfather. Since Jerry had never legally adopted his stepdaughter, he had no legal rights. He had assumed at the time of the divorce that he had visitation rights, but found to his horror that he did not. He had no legal relationship with his stepdaughter.

Because no legal relationship comes into existence between a stepparent and stepchild at the time the natural parent and stepparent marry, the stepparent has no legal hold on the child. If a stepparent does win custody in the case of the death of the natural parent, over the claims of the natural relatives, it is granted in the best interest of the child—not on the grounds of stepparents' rights. Stepparents are in a weak position in a custody fight because parental rights do not grow out of acting like a parent.

The stepparent who wishes to ensure visitation rights after a divorce from the stepchild's natural parent should consult a lawyer before the divorce. In the state of California, the law states that "in the discretion of the court, reasonable visitation rights may be granted to any other person having an interest in the welfare of the child."

It is true that there is no legal relationship between stepparent and stepchild. However, the stepparent may have an "equitable right" to see the stepchild. Divorce court is a court of equity. Part of the court's decisions concern protecting the children involved. If the stepparent can show extraordinary circumstances (such as parenting the stepchild for ten years, for example) and can show that not being allowed to see the child would be detrimental to the child, the stepparent may hope the court "invokes equitable jurisdiction." This would ask the judge to consider that visitation rights by the stepparent would be in the best interest of the child.

In all legal matters concerning the stepfamily, it is best to consult a lawyer who is knowledgeable in family law.

The Question of Adoption

Many stepfamilies will inevitably face the issue of adoption. Should a stepparent adopt the stepchildren? Or should the stepchildren retain their ties to the absentee natural parent? These questions can only be answered by the natural parents, stepparent, and children in the stepfamily.

Since each stepfamily has its own unique situation and needs, it is difficult to build a case for or against adoption by the stepparent. It is apparent, however, that adoption in the stepfamily is occurring with increasing frequency each year, and the courts are making the adoption process easier for the stepparent.

The advantages of adopting one's stepchildren are convincing. It gives the stepparent and stepchild a legal and permanent relationship. The stepparent gains the legal rights of a natural parent and the stepchild gains the legal rights of a natural child.

In addition to gaining legal security through adoption, the stepparent, parent, and child may also gain a sense of family security. Should the natural parent die, the adoptive stepparent would not have to fear losing custody of the child. The child may feel more secure about the future knowing that someone will be there to care for him or her. Adoption eliminates the presence of two different last names in the family and gives the children the same status within the family. It may also symbolize family unity; all members belong together in a family that is meant to be permanent.

In a blended family, with the permission of the ex-spouse,

it is possible to change the children's last names without a formal adoption procedure. Many parents choose to ask their child's view on the name changes.

The disadvantages of adoption are convincing, too. It eliminates the legal relationship between the child and the absentee parent; the absentee, natural parent relinquishes legal and emotional claims to the child. In addition, adoption may sever the child's ties to extended family members on the absentee parent's side of the family. By severing ties to the absentee, natural parent, many families may choose to sever relationships with that parent's relatives too. Adoption may also be harmful if the stepparent adopts from any motive other than the best interest of child and family. Adoption is not a tool of revenge or the glue that will bind the remarriage together forever.

The adoption issue may also create conflict between the parent and stepparent by raising such questions as, "But don't you want my child?" and, "But then we'll lose the support payments—and lawyers cost money."

The decision to adopt must be made only after careful consideration of the needs of child and stepparent. It is a decision that cannot be made lightly or in haste.

Financial Issues

Money can be one of the biggest battling issues in the stepfamily. The reasons for this are complex and depend upon the type of stepfamily.

One crucial factor is that one individual usually cannot adequately support two families. For example, consider the man who pays child support for his children who live with his ex-wife and is remarried to a woman who has children and is his stepfamily's sole support (either the ex-husband is deceased or his whereabouts are unknown). It's nearly impossible to avoid money hassles in this situation when the man earns an average income. His stepfamily may feel squeezed to live on the income left over after child support payments are made, and his children may feel squeezed living on the single parent's income plus child support. The child support is usually insufficient to pay for any "extras." The ex-wife may resent this and place pressure and demands on the ex-husband for increased child support. The present wife may feel guilty that her children are an extra financial burden. As you can see, the scenario for money hassles is present in this stepfamily situation.

This hassle is usually absent in families whose income is above average. Stepfamilies with higher than average incomes usually experience less conflict than those stepfamilies with average or low incomes.

Financial conflict may also be present within the stepfamily. Usually, allowances and school money create possible conflicts between stepsiblings and between parent and stepparent. Who gets how much and when are all decisions that may be decided upon by husband and wife. They could also be considered as negotiable items. Grievances concerning allowances and school money could very appropriately be issues to bring up for discussion at weekly family meetings.

Many stepparents and natural parents minimize financial conflicts by careful organization and documentation. They first consult a lawyer with expertise in the area of divorce or separation agreements, spousal support, and child support. Many stepparents and natural parents choose to maintain separately assets and incomes earned under their own name to avoid complications with their current spouse's ex-mate. In addition, they document carefully all money given to the ex-spouse for child support and any "extras" like that special prom dress, summer camp, set of clothes, and bicycle. Careful documentation can forestall future accusations.

Financially, almost all stepfamilies experience a need for careful budgeting. Deciding how much you have to spend, allocating resources appropriately, and identifying unnecessary expenses are all useful steps to preventing financial problems.

Planning Together

Planning together to form a successful, supportive stepfamily can involve planning prior to the remarriage and planning after the remarriage. Many couples may prefer to seek premarital counseling prior to the remarriage; others may prefer to seek professional help when problems begin to feel insurmountable. The crucial factor is this: The professional must be in tune with the unique problems experienced by stepfamilies.

A second aspect of planning involves *space* in the blended family. Frequently, many combination families find it economically necessary to live in a house previously lived in by one of the single-parent families. The unhappy result is that one family feels intruded upon, while the other family feels like it is visiting. The situation emphasizes two families rather than one stepfamily. Members oftentimes focus on what they are losing rather than on what they are gaining. When at all possible, stepfamilies may find this issue of space easier to deal with by moving to a new house. House-hunting together, finding a house, planning how to divide the space in the house—all of these ventures promote a feeling of cohesiveness between the family members. All start off as equals in the process of blending to form a stepfamily.

If this optimum move is financially impossible, then building an addition to the old house is, perhaps, the next best alternative. This second option enables the children who are moving into the "old" house to have their own "new and unused" space. They are then neither intruding nor made to feel like visitors.

Everyone in the stepfamily needs to have some space of his or her own. With their own space, members may feel more secure that they have a place in the family. They can then proceed to focus on the positive gains to be derived from the steprelationship.

A third aspect of planning concerns the involvement of the extended family members: grandparents, stepgrandparents, relatives, and steprelatives. Many stepfamilies complain of "too many fingers in the pie," yet the extended family can also be an asset to the stepfamily. Extended family relatives—natural and step—can reinforce the family guidelines and structure set up by the parent and stepparent. If relatives try to undermine this structure, parent and stepparent must be willing to confront them about the destructiveness of such behavior. The extended family can also provide support by taking the children for occasional weekend visits to allow the parent and stepparent some precious time alone.

A fourth aspect of planning involves providing for privacy in the stepfamily.

One thirty-seven-year-old stepfather was uncertain as to how to handle a lack of privacy in his stepfamily. His two young teen-age stepdaughters had lived with their mother alone for several years. Since they lived in a house of all women, they had grown very casual about wandering around in various stages of undress.

"I felt really uncomfortable when they wandered through the house in T-shirt and underwear; but I didn't know how to discuss this with my wife and stepdaughters without sounding weird...you know ...the old incest taboo. I finally decided to just risk telling them how I felt. To my relief, they readily agreed that, perhaps, they'd grown a little too casual living by themselves. Now the girls wear clothes or a robe, and I feel a lot better."

All members need to respect the privacy of other family members. This is especially important in a stepfamily that must deal with the maturing sexuality of teen-age children. Appropriate dress and respect for one another's privacy should be clearly defined.

A final aspect of planning concerns being realistic about time and instant results. Most individuals minimize the negative aspects and hard work involved in blending two families. Their expectations lead them to expect *instant results*—a perfect steprelationship. A healthy steprelationship takes time to build and nurture. With time, members in the stepfamily can explore new ways of dealing with problems *as a family*.

Too often, one of two things happens to prevent the stepfamily from dealing with problems as they occur. One parent may try to carry the total responsibility for success or failure alone. One cannot—it is a cooperative responsibility.

The stepfamily may try to single out one individual in the family system as "the problem." No one individual can carry the total responsibility for any one problem. The problem does not lie with the individual, it lies in the family relationships, and between family members. Members must be able to deal with problems *as a family*. Again, it is a cooperative responsibility involving all members of the stepfamily. All must work together to achieve success.

Guidelines for Stepfamily Planning

1. *Seek professional help.* If you feel that professional counseling either prior to the remarriage or after the remarriage would be beneficial, don't hesitate to seek a professional, trained, and qualified psychologist or marriage, family, and child counselor. Be sure to determine that the professional is trained in dealing with the problems unique to stepfamilies.

2. *Attend stepparenting courses, if available.* Four years ago, the first course for stepfamilies was offered in the state of California. "Stepfamilies, a Cooperative Responsibility"— which was the basis for this book—is a course designed to explore the needs and expectations of the stepfamily in order to bring about more cohesive stepfamily relations. Since then, the course has been offered at numerous colleges and universities throughout the state with great success. Individuals interested in a course on stepparenting should check with their local university or community college to determine if such a course is offered via extension or other programs.

3. *Get support.* Remarried couples can meet others with similar problems by joining one of the growing number of organizations for remarrieds. For example, the ten-year-old Remarrieds, Inc., has thirty-one chapters in twenty states. Executive Director Howard Samuelson says the group helps couples to get going again socially and assists in establishing a more stable family life in remarriage through programs that are social, educational, and cultural. Program emphasis in most chapters is on social activities, although educational speakers, discussions, and community activities are also regularly scheduled. "Remarrieds, Inc., is meeting a real need

by exploring the problem areas in remarriage which are unique or more complicated than in first marriages—mixing families, stepchildren, the former mate, mixed financial affairs, and communications problems," says Samuelson. For further information, interested couples may write to Remarrieds, Inc., P.O. Box 742, Santa Ana, CA 92702.

Stepfamily Foundation of California is a California-based organization offering similar services to stepfamilies. It is a nonprofit, educational corporation that was founded in 1977 to be an active advocate for stepfamilies. The foundation provides a support network, sponsors discussion groups, and offers public education programs to family members. For information, interested individuals may write Stepfamily Foundation of California, Inc., 900 Welch Road, Suite 400, Palo Alto, CA 94304.

There are a number of other types of self-help groups that may assist members of stepfamilies or those who might become part of a stepfamily to deal with some of the related issues of family relations, child rearing, health, and the like. They are part of a growing movement of self-help mutual aid groups that enable people with particular problems to assist each other in dealing with these problems.

A substantial listing of such groups, along with a discussion of how to form them and how professionals can work with them, is to be found in *Help: A Working Guide to Self-Help Groups,* by Alan Gartner and Frank Riessman of the National Self-Help Clearinghouse; published by New Viewpoints (a division of Franklin Watts). The Clearinghouse is located at the City University Graduate Center, 33 West 42 Street, New York, N.Y. 10036.

References

Arnold, Eugen, M.D. *Helping Parents Help Their Children.* New York: Brunner and Mazel, 1978.

Bach, George, and Wyden, Peter. *The Intimate Enemy.* New York: Avon Books, 1970.

Baer, Jean. *The Second Wife.* New York: Pyramid Books, 1972.

Bernard, Jessie. *The Future of Marriage.* New York: Bantam Books, 1972.

Bowlby, J. *Attachment and Loss,* Separation, Anxiety and Anger, vol. II. New York: Basic Books, 1973.

Briggs, Dorothy Corkille. *Your Child's Self-Esteem.* New York: Dolphin Books, 1970.

Farber, Bernard, ed. *Kinship and Family Organizations.* New York: John Wiley and Sons, Inc., 1966.

Fast, I., and Cain, A. "The Stepparent Role: Potential for Disturbances in Family Functioning," *American Journal of Orthopsychiatry,* vol. XXXI (April 1966): 485–491.

Fisher, E.O. *Divorce: The New Freedom, A guide to Divorce and Divorce Counseling.* San Francisco: Harper & Row, 1974.

Furman, Erna. *A Child's Parent Dies,* New Haven and London: Yale University Press, 1974.

Ginott, Haim. *Between Parent and Child,* New York: Macmillan, 1965.

——*Between Parent and Teenager,* New York: Avon Books, 1969.

Goldstein, J., Freud, A., and Solnit, J. *Beyond the Best Interests of the Child,* New York: Free Press, 1973.

Keniston, Kenneth, and The Carnegie Council on Children. *All Our Children,* New York and London: Harcourt, Brace, Jovanovich; New York: Carnegie Corporation, 1977.

Kessler, S. *The American Way of Divorce: Prescription for Change,* Chicago: Nelson-Hall, 1975.

Lewis, M. *Clinical Aspects of Child Development.* Philadelphia: Lea and Febiger, 1971.

Lidz, Theodore, "The Family," *The Person,* New York: Basic Books, 1968, chap. two, pp. 54-67.

Maddox, Brenda, *The Half Parent,* New York: Signal Publishing, 1976.

Porteus, H. S. *Sex and Identity,* New York: Bobbs-Merrill, 1972.

Richards, Arlene and Wills, Irene. *How to Get It Together When Your Parents Are Coming Apart,* New York: Bantam Books, 1976.

Roman, Mel and Haddad, William. "The Case for Joint Custody," *Psychology Today,* September, 1978.

Roosevelt, R. and Lofas, J. *Living in Step,* New York: Stein and Day, 1976.

Ross, Elisabeth Kubler, *On Death and Dying,* New York: Macmillan, 1969.

Satir, Virginia. *Peoplemaking,* Palo Alto, Calif.: Science and Behavior Books, 1972.

Simon, A.W. *Stepchild In The Family, A View Of The Child In Remarriage,* New York: Odyssey Press, 1964.

Smith, William Carlson. *The Stepchild,* Chicago: The University of Chicago Press, 1953.

Wernick, Robert. *The Family,* New York: Time-Life Books, 1974.

Wood, Paul, M.D. and Swartz, Bernard. *How to Get Your Children to Do What You Want Them to Do;* Englewood Cliffs, N.J.: Prentice-Hall, 1977.

Zuckerman, Harold F. *Adolescence Is a Required Course.* Morristown, N.J.: General Learning Press, 1976.

Index